Doctor in the Zoo

*"I am a little bored. But if you tame me, it will
be as if the sun came to shine on my life. I shall
know the sound of a step that will be different
from all the others. Other steps send me hurrying
back underneath the ground. Yours will call me,
like music, out of my burrow. And then look:
do you see the grainfields down yonder? I do not
eat bread. Wheat is of no use to me. The wheat
fields have nothing to say to me. And that is sad.
But you have hair that is the color of gold. The
grain, which is also golden, will bring me back
the thought of you. And I shall love to listen to
the wind in the wheat. . . ."*

ANTOINE DE SAINT-EXUPÉRY, *THE LITTLE PRINCE.*

Doctor in the Zoo

Bruce Buchenholz

Introduction by Cleveland Amory

A Studio Book

The Viking Press

New York

TO ALL MY LOVED ONES, TWO-FOOTED
AND FOUR-FOOTED.

Introduction

Zoos are coming in for hard scrutiny these days. The Fund for Animals, for example, the anti-cruelty society of which I am president, takes a dim view of zoos. In my book, *Man Kind?*, I have hard words not only for such awful zoos as New York's Central Park Zoo—which has at least an excuse for being awful— but also such relatively inexcusably awful zoos as the Los Angeles Zoo and the San Francisco Zoo.

Some zoos' idea of "education" must be seen to be believed. At the Racine Zoo in Wisconsin, for example, I took pictures not of the animals but of the signs below their cages. Under "Siberian Tiger" the sign reads: "Usefulness: Pelts for Decorative Purposes." Under "African Lion" the sign reads: "Usefulness: Pelts & Rugs." Under "Syrian Brown Bear" the sign was: "Usefulness: Hide for Rugs, Meat for Food." Finally, under "Chimpanzee," the sign was simply: "Usefulness: Pets When Young—Zoo and Circus."

Such an organization should perhaps itself have a sign. Under "Zoo," I would suggest: "Usefulness: None."

Here and there, however, there are outstanding zoos, and one of these, surely, is New York's Bronx Zoo. William Conway, its director, seems to get most of the credit, but credit is also due to some other truly remarkable men under him. One of these is Dr. F. Wayne King, Director of Conservation and Environmental Education. Another is Dr. Joseph Davis, Scientific Assistant to the Director.

Add to these now another, a young man named Emil Dolensek, the hero of *Doctor in the Zoo*. A veterinarian, he is at the same time a very special veterinarian. And not just because his specialty is not your dog or your cat but zoo animals.

He is special also because of the way he looks at his profession. Take, for example, the way he talks about it. "The hardest thing," he says, "is the responsibility. Every time I handle an animal, I'm causing him distress, discomfort, fright, pain, perhaps even death. I always hope I'm right to do it, but sometimes I'm wrong."

Dr. Dolensek is clearly not just another veterinarian. He is truly an animal person. And I define an animal person as a person concerned not only with studying animals but also with doing something about man's inhumanity to them.

And just as Dr. Dolensek is not just another veterinarian, this book is not just another zoo book. It is a very different kind of zoo book indeed. The main reason is that you, the reader, are a vital part of it. And this is as it should be, because, as photographer Bruce Buchenholz reminds us in his preface, "you are animal too."

Dr. Buchenholz, a psychiatrist as well as a photographer, spent two years at the Bronx Zoo getting these pictures. And yet he has made you, the reader, almost as important as the animals themselves. You will see them through another you—your stand-in, Dr. Dolensek. And you will be made intimately aware—either painfully or humorously, as the case may be—that the situations in this book and the pictures of them are happening to part of you and your "family."

And this too needs a definition. For what you are seeing here is not just the "Family of Man," as we are so conceitedly inclined to call it, but your own much bigger and more important family —the family of us all, the Family of Animal.

In the Bronx Zoo there is a famous sign. "You are looking," it says, "at the most dangerous predator on earth." The sign is over a mirror. Think about it as you read this book. And the next time you see a "trophy" head on the wall, or hear a hunter boast of his exploits, think about it again. And the next time you see a woman in a wild fur coat—or a man, for that matter—think about it still a third time.

CLEVELAND AMORY

ACKNOWLEDGMENTS: I take some comfort from the thought that the book is an obvious appreciation of the people in it.

My debt to Emil Dolensek goes far beyond the cooperation and infinite patience one gleans from the pictures. When I needed access, he got it for me. When I needed information, he gave it. When I needed transportation, he provided it. When I needed cheering up, he cheered. When I needed putting down, he put. One time there was a picture I was especially eager to get. Emil knew I could best take it from the top of some large cages perched on a rocky hill. On that day I had rather severe neuritis in my right arm that rendered me quite helpless. Without a word he hauled me up that rocky hill, hoisted me onto the roof of the cages, and pointed me right at the picture. Afterward he commented: "Well, that's the first one we really had to work hard for." I was so grateful for that "we"! Often in the text that follows I casually provide some bit of interesting information about an animal or an arcane piece of natural history lore. Nine times out of ten that's Emil speaking. I might have done a similar book without Emil, but it wouldn't have been this book, and it wouldn't have been the adventure of love that, in fact, it was.

It's no exaggeration to say that I met no one at the zoo who wasn't friendly, warm, and helpful. Joe Lombard, Keeper at the hospital, promptly accepted me as a friend and was always ready and willing to help in any way he could. Jim Coder, Head Keeper at the hospital, has more experience than anybody else there, handles the animals beautifully, and was always ready when something was needed. Virginia D'Agos-

8

tino and Carlos Estol, pathology technicians, were more than hospitable and made the hospital a very pleasant home for me during the many months I spent there.

The other veterinarians with whom I worked, Roy Bellhorn, Alan Belson, and Jay Hyman, were unfailingly considerate and friendly. Gráinne Browne made everything exciting; she has that rarest of talents, the gift of love.

It's difficult to name the zoo people who put themselves out for me—they were too many. I would guess that Jim Doherty, Assistant Curator of Mammals, put up with more than most. Joe Ruf, Animal Manager in the Mammal Department, Pete Brazaitis, Assistant Animal Manager in the Reptile Department, and Bob Brandner, Keeper in the Reptile Department, were some of my most helpful and kindest friends. William Flynn, Curator of the Aquarium, was especially gracious.

My gratitude to the Bronx Zoo is tinged with anxiety. As is often the case, objective data can be subjectively interpreted—with opposite inferences drawn. One could look at these pictures and say: "See how carefully the Bronx Zoo guards the health of its animals," or, "See how much sickness there is in the Bronx Zoo collection." The latter inference is completely false. I'd be greatly distressed if the material as a whole was not seen as a tribute to the institution. My intention was not to give a picture of the Bronx Zoo, or even a segment of its operation, but rather to use these as a vehicle to carry my thesis. I am, nevertheless, anxiously aware that the part can be taken for the whole, false and destructive conclusions can be drawn, material can be misinterpreted and mis-

9

used. I have made a book about the relationship between man and animals and the inherent emotional factors. My experience in doing so has incidentally but clearly convinced me that the Bronx Zoo is one of the world's great humane, scientific, and educational institutions.

While the zoo was putting up with my presence, my family was putting up with my absence. I like to think that the latter was more difficult. One day recently when I arrived home, my two-year-old son, Peter, who used to greet me with an effusive "Daddy! Daddy!", calmly walked into the kitchen and announced to my wife, Gretchen: "That's a man." Nicole, eight years old, declared acidly: "It'll be nice to have a man around the house." The mastiff puppy made it clear that "he doesn't *smell* like a man." Seven-year-old Christopher, the patient one with the long memory, said: "*Now* can we go to the Empire State Building?" Each had his say, but Gretchen stood up for me nobly. It was noble because she'd been bearing alone the considerable burden of a considerable household for many, many months. She'd also been encouraging me, providing moral support, giving me ideas and valuable suggestions, and reacting very knowledgeably to the pictures and text. No matter how pressing her immediate responsibilities were, she made herself available when I needed her help.

I'm lucky that Barbara Burn is my friend. If she were just my editor it wouldn't have worked. Even though editors as a species are a step nearer the angels than ordinary mortals, it wouldn't have worked. With wit, affability, great good nature, and infinite patience Barbara guided, supported, and pushed me along the path to publication.

And I don't take kindly to guidance or support, much less pushing. But I take kindly to Barbara.

I cannot close this without acknowledging that Charles Reynolds, Picture Editor of *Popular Photography,* suggested this book, and, in fact, that I might not have done it without his urging.

I am an abominable typist. Nancy Buchenholz, who is as skillful as I am inept, took that burden from me when she could ill afford the time or energy.

Many people have given me a great deal. When my equipment was stolen, Iris and Ernst Auerbacher and Bunny and Milton Rattner made it possible for me to re-equip myself and proceed with my work.

Obviously I have much to be grateful for. Most of all I am grateful for the wonderful gift of friendship.

He tossed the empty syringe into a metal can and lifted from the treatment table the warm furry body of a little lion cub. Holding it cradled in his arms, he walked slowly down the corridor. His face was expressionless, but his eyes were very weary, and there was a tiny monotonous twitch at the corner of his mouth. He continued his slow walk to the morgue at the end of the passage. He carefully placed the body on a table, turned, and walked back down the corridor, alone.

You may not have daily responsibility for life or death, yet this book is about you. You won't realize this if you glance quickly through the pictures, but if you have the patience to linger with some of them you may get a sense of what I mean. You will respond to these animals, and you will find that they are deeply meaningful to you. Our feelings for animals are very deep and very old.

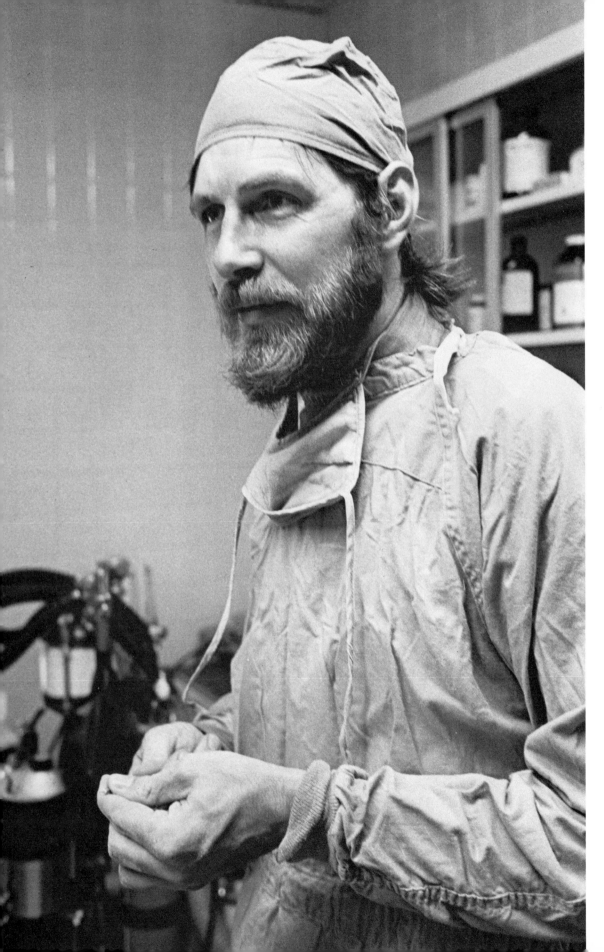

"The hardest thing is the responsibility. Every time I handle an animal I'm causing him distress—discomfort, fright, pain, perhaps even death. I always hope I'm right to do it, but sometimes I'm wrong."
—DR. EMIL DOLENSEK

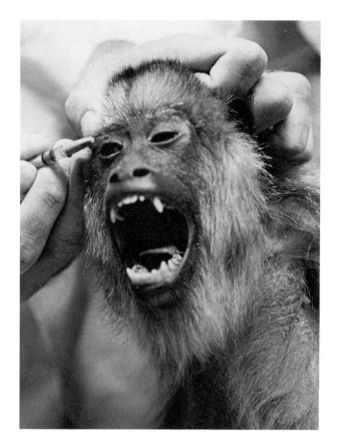

Since man is himself an animal, he shares basic biological characteristics with all animals. One aspect of this biological sharing is the emotional realm. Reptiles, birds, and mammals will show reasonably clear emergency emotions, such as fear and anger, as well as signs of pleasure. I recall once attending a dinner given at the Central Park Zoo by the Friends of the Zoo, where a few tame animals were brought to amuse the diners. I was especially impressed by a large pebbly-skinned lizard because it was among the ugliest beasts I'd ever seen. I soon discovered, however, that when scratched under the chin the animal would stretch his neck out to the scratching hand, close his eyes, and compose his features into what on a human being (if you could find one with such a face) would clearly be a smile. It made me feel warm and friendly toward him, and I was able to see that there was great beauty in what I had at first thought ugly.

Most human beings have a more or less conscious sense of relatedness to all living creatures, an ability to identify with them, and many tend to project onto animals their own emotional reactions. This can be observed in very young children, who seem to make no distinction between pets and other members of the family. Most of us can remember that, when quite young, we had fantasies involving animal friends with whom we had strange and marvelous adventures. Even earlier in life we may have had an animal toy that exerted a magically comforting and soothing effect. At about that time our minds were filled with stories about the cow that jumped over the moon, Mother Goose's gander, Little Miss Muffet's spider, and many others.

For purposes of this book the important fact is that each individual human being has within him the germ of complex emotional relationships with animals. Some sense of all this is expressed in numerous age-old myths containing instances of the fundamental significance of animals in the emotional life of mankind. The Bible is, of course, the source of many stories in which animals figure. It is, in fact, difficult to imagine how the Bible would have turned out had there not been that snake right at the beginning. Perhaps closer to our daily lives are the popular media, which cater to our emotional needs with legendary heroes (and heroines) such as Rin-Tin-Tin, Lassie, and Flipper the porpoise. And we have *Planet of the Apes, Pogo,* and the whole Walt Disney empire to remind us that animals play a major role in our unconscious fantasy life.

More immediately, and more personally, there is our dream relationship with animals. Most people are well aware that dreams are significant products of each person's emotional life. Haven't you had dreams in which animals figured? Perhaps you've ridden a winged horse or been carried through the sky by an enormous bird or made friends with a powerful jungle beast. Have you ever, in your dreams, been taking care of some little furry creatures who were menaced by a grave danger? Turtles, snakes, and spiders also figure prominently in dreams. In your dreams these animals have symbolic significance,

but the fact that animals serve as symbols in widely disparate societies implies that there is a basic, primal emotional relationship between animals and man. You are a part of this in a very personal sense. Even if animals play no part in your daily life, they are within you and are part of you.

Each person, depending on his life experiences and life circumstances, is more or less in touch with these aspects of his inner emotional life. Most people who have some sense of this satisfy their needs by taking one or more pets into their household and incorporating them into their family. This is such an age-old and universal custom that it is, in itself, sufficient witness to the depth of our need. The individual human family sponsors, takes responsibility for,

and adds to its group one or more members of the less favored and more helpless species. Anyone's helplessness is of great importance to us. Notice how people, how you yourself, respond to puppies, kittens, and other baby animals. Notice how you feel when confronted with an animal that is suffering and in pain. Watch for this response as you go through this book. It may be hard at first to think of an enormous Himalayan snow leopard as helpless, but if he were not he wouldn't be in that cage or living precariously in the wild in constant terror of man.

Human response to animal helplessness is a compound reaction composed of guilt, compassion, and the fundamental shared helplessness of all living creatures. We share with every animal the basic experiences of being born, of living, and of dying. And any experience of helplessness, direct or indirect, brings closer to us the terrifying specter of death.

Another important response we have to animals is essentially an aesthetic one. The capacity for aesthetic response varies from person to person, but few of us are totally unmoved by the grace of the big cats or the brilliant plumage of tropical birds. As one goes through the list of species, it becomes clear that each kind of animal evokes its particular group of emotional reactions. We tend to choose as pets the particular animal from which we expect greatest satisfaction of our own special needs.

There are some people in whom the animal aspect of their emotional make-up is sufficiently pressing for them to be inclined to give animals a major role in their lives. They may work, professionally or as volunteers, in animal-care or welfare organizations, zoos, game preserves, wildlife conservation groups, and the like. Such people are readily identified: They obviously *care* about animals. Every human being pictured in this book falls into that category. They are all experiencing basic emotional reactions and primitive stirrings that are, however well you may hide them, part of your own make-up. To help you realize some part of this emotional constellation in yourself, Dr. Emil Dolensek will represent "you" in these pictures. Watch him closely, because this book is largely about him, and so, largely, about you. There are other people in the book, most of them in situations you might try to imagine yourself a part of. And there are some pictures of animals you can confront directly, without the intervention of a surrogate.

Since Emil Dolensek is your stand-in, I should tell you something about him. He is the Chief Veterinarian at the New York Zoological Park, usually called the Bronx Zoo. Situated in the heart of a crowded metropolis, the zoo is a very beautiful 252-acre park of woodland, fields, and streams. It houses some 1500 birds, about 560 snakes and reptiles, and at least 784 mammals. This is one of the world's great zoos, and many of the exhibits represent the latest word in wild-animal housing. The African Plains, the South American Plains, the World of Birds, for example, are marvels of created environments. Good zoo people are, however, always searching for still better ways, and consequently good zoos are in a constant state of flux. Emil is vitally concerned with these matters, since details of the environment materially affect the health of its inhabitants. One obvious example, not uncommon at the Bronx Zoo, is that when an environment is so well established the birth rate of its inhabitants increases greatly. Pretty soon the environment contains many more animals than it can optimally accommodate, and the animals start to show a decreased resistance to disease. The curators and keepers keep a constant eye on each individual in their charge, promptly reporting any deviation from the norm, change in accustomed behavior, or apparent pathology. In addition to this, Emil makes his own daily rounds, slowly riding past each exhibit. Even when there is no apparent pathology, animals are subjected to periodic health checks and, in some instances, periodic immunizations. Of necessity, emphasis is heavily on "public health" and preventive medicine. Despite all this, there is a

need for direct treatment, much of it surgical. But if Emil treats a bird's broken wing, for example, he always asks, "Why did it happen?"

So beautiful a zoo, with such a large variety of animals attractively presented, draws enormous crowds of visitors, about two and a half million each year. Visitors do not, however, affect significantly the health of the residents. Although some people persist in feeding the animals, this breach of the rules,

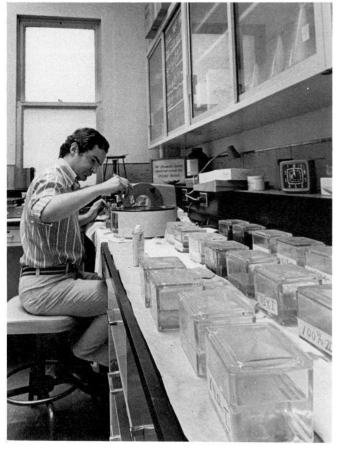

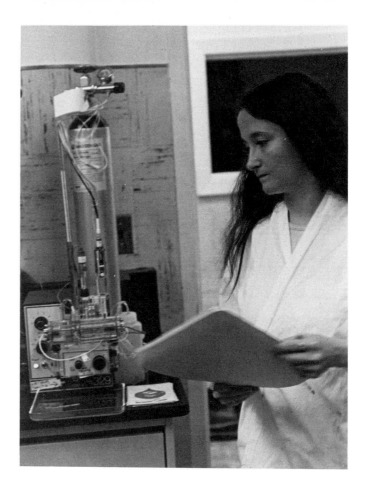

though it never does any good, is a surprisingly uncommon source of trouble. Problems are more likely to arise from objects other than food thrown or falling into the enclosures. When, for example, one animal who died of old age was autopsied, fourteen rubber balls were found in his stomach. Constant attention is also given to prevention of diseases carried by outside animals. Dogs, cats, and other pets are, of course, not admitted to the park. Animals shipped into the zoo or passing through for one reason or another are held in quarantine until proved free of communicable dis-

ease. Incoming food and its preparation must also be carefully supervised, and so must the general cleanliness of the quarters.

Many of these matters of hygiene can be, and are, left confidently in the hands of the trained, experienced, and knowledgeable curators with their staffs of keepers. But Emil can never forget that he shares with the curators the responsibility for the health of all the animals. The curators are the officials who have over-all responsibility for the various divisions in the zoo, and they make all major decisions within their areas. There

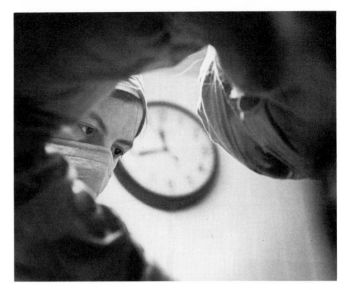

is, therefore, at the Bronx Zoo, a Curator of Mammals, a Curator of Birds, and a Curator of Reptiles, each of whom may have an Assistant Curator. The keepers are usually assigned to specific buildings or compounds—that is, to a specific group of animals and their quarters. They are in close daily contact with their charges and directly responsible for the physical care of the animals and their enclosures. The keepers are immediately supervised by Animal Managers and Assistant Animal Managers.

Emil's headquarters is the animal hospital, a rambling one-story building in the same constant process of improvement as the zoo itself. At the moment it consists of a ward and quarantine area, a treatment room equipped for surgery and X-ray, a clinical pathology laboratory, a tissue pathology laboratory, a stockroom, a nursery for the very young animals, the doctors' office, and a record room. The equipment is superb, the laboratories replete with complex machines to aid in studies of all body fluids and for preparation of histological and fluid specimens. The treatment room gleams with the polished chrome of an operating table, instruments for just about any procedure that might be required, an anesthesia machine, an electrocardiogram machine, an X-ray machine, and rows of sterilized packs. The spacious nursery has a large observation window, an incubator, scales, a playpen, and all the miscellaneous paraphernalia of just about any well-equipped nursery. Perhaps the most interesting thing about the treatment room and the stockroom is the range of sizes of the instruments and equipment. From a tiny bird to an enormous orangutan, all can be, and often are, treated in the same day.

Because of the zoo's location in a large metropolitan community, Emil has a large staff of veterinary and other medical specialists available to help him when special problems are encountered. In addition, a part-time veterinary pathologist studies every animal who dies in the zoo, not only to determine the cause of death but also to make collections of tissues and other specimens, which provide invaluable material for the study of comparative pathology. Careful record-keeping and the patient accumulation of specimens, slides, and data constitute an exceedingly valuable body of information. Compared to the library of volumes available on dogs and cats, horses and cattle, published information on specific exotic animals is quite inadequate. Emil often finds himself treading unknown territory.

Fortunately, Emil has on his staff a tissue-pathology technician, Carlos Estol, and a clinical-pathology technician, Ginny D'Agostino, each of whom has the unusual expertise and devotion that enable the hospital to keep up with the tremendous flow of material. Each day there are tissues to be prepared for microscopic study from biopsies or autopsied animals, blood, urine, and stool specimens from sick animals, as well as similar specimens from quarantined animals and from those having their periodic routine health examinations. Laboratory work plays an increasingly important role in medicine, especially when there is so much emphasis on preventive medicine. You will notice in a number of the pictures that Emil is taking blood samples for study.

The roster of staff that helps Emil in his work is supplemented by a volunteer parasitologist, Dr. Lucy Clausen, and in

24

the summer by a series of advanced veterinary students. For the past couple of years Gráinne Browne, a senior student at the Veterinary College in Dublin, has assisted Emil through the summers. You'll see her in many of the pictures.

Despite the beautiful equipment and the well-rounded staff, Emil can't get as much done as he'd like. He tries to be at the zoo from 8:30 or 9:00 A.M. to about 5:00 P.M., Monday through Friday, but the work day rarely ends as planned, the five-day work week often becomes six and occasionally even seven. One sequence of pictures represents a situation that kept Emil at the hospital around the clock for three consecutive days. And, of course, he's always on call in case of emergency.

Here is Emil working too hard, with too much responsibility and inadequate time, for a fraction of the earnings he could gain in private veterinary practice. Why? Because he has to. He has been in private practice and came to the zoo from a large suburban practice. The work at the zoo admirably fulfills pressing inner needs that even Emil himself is only dimly aware of. In a way, Emil and the animal kingdom belong together. Beyond the difference in hours and remuneration, there are many other obvious differences between a suburban veterinary practice and responsibility for a large zoo, and these differences offer some clues to Emil's personality. In his characteristic self-deprecating way Emil is likely to suggest that perhaps he likes the glamour and authority at the zoo. That's probably true, because he has a very human mixture of self-doubt and vanity. But I think there are more cogent factors. I think, for example, that the animals one treats in private practice

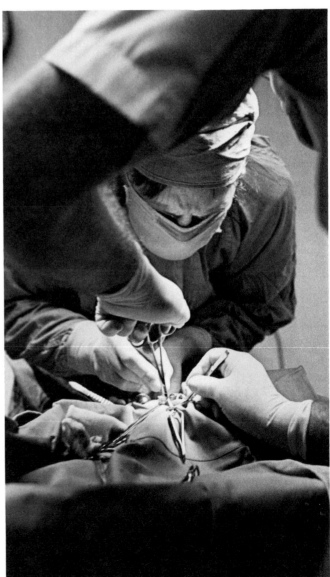

belong to the people who bring them. The veterinarian's relationship to the animals is predicated on their illnesses, limited to their treatment, and controlled by their owners. The zoo, on the other hand, has a large group of the animal kingdom with which Emil is in daily contact over a long period of time. You can see from the pictures that Emil forms deep relationships with the animals — more than that, it's perfectly obvious that he loves them. I believe it's as simple as that: He loves them so much that he can't leave them.

There are, of course, ancillary factors. The variety inherent in Emil's work has great appeal, and there's a tremendous challenge in doing work unsupported by a voluminous literature. Emil likes to meet challenges with animals. Since these are wild animals, that may sound like a dangerous proposition. Emil, however, tends to test himself in professional ways rather than take absurd chances. He has too much respect for the animals and too much understanding of them to get in their way in the wrong circumstances. In his daily rounds he often stops to give a few kind words to the larger and more volatile animals because, as he says "I never know under what circumstances I'll meet them next." The fact of the matter is, however, that even if he didn't have a

28

healthy fear where fear is appropriate, Emil would still stop for friendly interchanges.

In watching Emil work, one notices many things. He handles animals with great tenderness and respect. He is outstandingly competent professionally and has a keen scientific curiosity. He feels a deep sense of responsibility, yet he is confident and calm. His special medical interest is anesthesiology, and he has done a great deal of research with the tranquilizing drugs that can immobilize large animals and make it possible to work easily with them. He is currently testing some experimental materials that promise much in the way of efficacy, speed, and safety. Roy Bellhorn, the ophthalmologist, tells about the early days of testing when he was examining the retina of a young tiger tranquilized with one of the newly received drugs.

There is still wonder in Roy's voice as he describes looking through his fundus camera (an instrument for examining and photographing the interior of the eye) at the tiger's retina, and then his sudden, stunning realization that the retina wasn't there. The retina wasn't there, the eye wasn't there, the tiger wasn't there! Looking up in confusion, Roy saw his patient staggering toward Joe, the hospital keeper, who was busily engaged with a medical bag. Roy shouted. Joe looked up. Joe and the tiger faced each other briefly—and both collapsed.

Talking about special interests, I suppose it is very natural that even Emil, with his encompassing feeling for animals, should have favorites. In conversation one can mention almost any species and Emil is likely to remark, with feeling, "They're *nice* animals!" It's my impression, however, that he has a special

place in his heart for the big cats and for all baby mammals, which is why the longest sequence in the book concerns a mother tiger and her cub. Aside from these groups, there are many individuals who are his special friends, many of them animals who have spent a good deal of time in the hospital. Whenever Emil walks through the South American Plains exhibit, there is a guanaco who follows close behind, frequently nudging him for attention. This guanaco spent part of her early childhood in Emil's home, and Emil likes to tell how he taught her to walk. It's also quite a sight to see a huge Siberian tiger come bounding over at Emil's call and submit pleasurably to having its chin scratched. Some time ago there was a jaguar in the hospital whose menacing snarls and growls intimidated all who came near. When its cage was opened, the large cat

would spring like a shot—right into Emil's arms. Emil loves these signs of reciprocated affection and takes pride in them, but then who wouldn't? Some of the animals are wary of the doctor, usually those he has "knocked down" several times (injected with a tranquilizer by means of a carbon-dioxide pistol). He seems a little embarrassed and rueful about this but accepts it with good grace and exercises a special sensitivity with these particular animals.

Despite the depth of his relationship with the animals, Emil refuses to anthropomorphize. The more intensely one cares about animals, the more earnestly one wishes to relate to them and the more one is tempted to understand them by the most readily available means—one's understanding of human beings. To a limited extent this

attitude is valid. As I suggested earlier, man shares with other animals certain basic emotions. It is, for example, reasonable to assume that an animal who flees is afraid and one who attacks is angry. Many animals show clearly recognizable pleasure responses, and most people who have lived with puppies have seen their pets act in an obviously guilty manner. But the outward manifestations of complex and subtle emotions are often expressed in gestures and attitudes that are specific. As one example from among very many, the owl-like frogmouth bird will draw himself up erect and rigid, raising his head so that his beak points straight up. He looks haughty and disdainful, but he's not. He is afraid. In fact, he's hiding. In natural surroundings he looks like part of a tree, although in an open cage space he looks a little silly.

These specific gestures and attitudes can be learned by close observation, but only if one can observe open-mindedly, without preconception or prejudice. Nevertheless, many animals show readable emotional reactions, and you will recognize the feelings of some of the animals in the pictures. The real trouble comes when one is tempted to say things like, "He doesn't like the red feeding dish—the color is too bright for him," or, worse, "He loves children so much that he doesn't mind what they do to him." In other words, while there may be reasonable cues as to what an animal is feeling, it's pretty difficult to know what he is thinking. Emil knows animals well enough to understand them on their own terms, and he is well enough adjusted not to be pressed to project onto the animals his own emotional problems and needs.

It is not easy to give a picture of Emil's

"typical" day. Almost anything can happen, and one could say: "That's typical." Snakes with abscesses, birds with broken bones, a penguin with pneumonia, a tapir with an infected jaw, a buffalo with diarrhea, newborn animals whose mothers neglect them, a pregnant gorilla who can't deliver her fetus, big cats with virus infections, animals confiscated by the inspection agencies, injured or sick animals from the airport, new arrivals for the zoo collections—on and on they come in an endless stream thoughout the year. If one is prepared for anything, the preparations are never in vain. All the animals are smoothly and warmly received, housed, fed, processed, cared for, and, when appropriate, dispatched to their proper destinations. On one "typical" day the hospital housed a couple of Asiatic lion cubs which had been detained at the airport ASPCA shelter for several sweltering days in a tiny metal-lined crate. They were pitiful by the time someone thought to send them to the hospital, dehydrated, suffering from heat exhaustion, covered with abrasions from their efforts to escape their box. It wasn't long, however, before they were completely recovered, romping and frolicking and practicing looking regal, just as six-month-old lion cubs should. In the next cage was a young giant anteater, a new arrival for the zoo's collection. Unlike many of his kind, this fellow was very friendly indeed and eagerly met the visitor's exploring finger with his own exploring nose. This one spent a lot of time sleeping, head and tail curled beneath him so that he looked like a large clump of black-and-white straw. His neighbors were a couple of capybaras, which look to me like gigantic guinea pigs. (One summer we had at

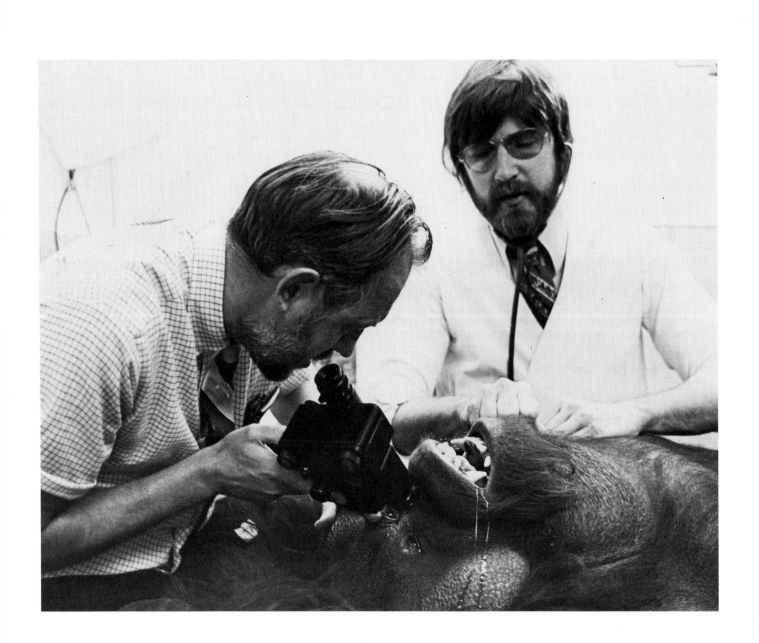

home a guinea pig on loan from my daughter's classroom. I entertained the fantasy of somehow borrowing a capybara just long enough to take it to the teacher in September, saying, "Look how Gwendolyn thrived over the summer!" and to walk out without another word.) There was a broad-winged hawk with a dropped wing which seemed pleased to grace any wrist offered for it to perch on, and which showed an unusual and touching trust in all human beings. The last cage in that ward housed a huge jaguar, which had, en route to Bengal, almost chewed his way through a metal-lined, three-quarter-inch-plywood crate.

He tore himself up quite a bit in the process, but that crate didn't look so good either. He was about fifteen minutes away from freedom and newspaper headlines when his plot was discovered and he was shipped to the hospital for rest and recuperation. Another section of smaller cages contained a confiscated ocelot which was as friendly as a pussy, a young frogmouth, a tame ferret, and a little flying squirrel which spent the day totally buried in a clump of newspapers. The nursery had recently been vacated by Patty-cake, a baby gorilla from the Central Park Zoo; she had stayed until her broken arm was well healed. On this day it housed the tiger cub pictured in the sequence at the end of this book.

A review of the hospital patients, therefore, is a fixed part of Emil's day. When he arrives in the morning, he may find directives from the administration or reports from the curators calling to his attention matters they feel he should follow up. This is often followed by a round of the zoo during which he looks over the animals, compares notes with the curators and keepers, and plans with them for any procedures that involve their charges. Other routines include immunizations, collection of body-fluid specimens for study, and regular meetings with the professional staff of the zoo.

The afternoon might be devoted to planned procedures. A shipment of snakes might have to be examined and specimens taken for laboratory study. Or an orangutan might be due for his regular checkup (physical examination, X-rays, blood and feces study, and sometimes, if the ophthalmologist is available, special eye studies). Or follow-up exams might have to be done on treated animals which have been sent back to their compounds. There are always a number of "out-patients" to be treated; animals are removed from their environments and brought to the hospital for treatment only when it is clearly necessary. As you will see in the photographs, a yak can be given a tuberculin test in the field, but an alligator must be X-rayed in the hospital.

These are daily routines that can rarely be neglected. To get a more accurate picture of a day, one has to imagine that they are interspersed with and constantly interrupted by all sorts of unforeseen happenings.

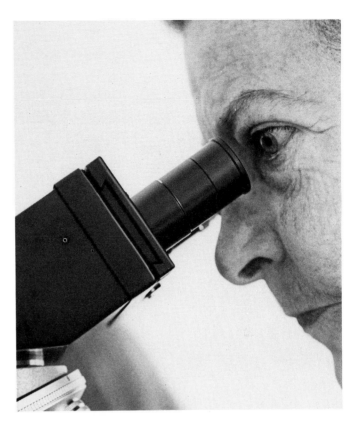

The pictures in the book are arranged, sometimes quite arbitrarily, into days of the week. While any particular incident may not really have happened on a Monday, for example, it could have. The Monday pictures show what a Monday might well be like, and so too for the other days. The Friday story ends in a seventy-two-hour saga, which happens every once in a while. In all, the photographs add up to a realistic picture of Emil's work week, although somewhat heavily loaded in order to encompass more material. It must be made clear that the zoo's collection is remarkably healthy and that, in fact, fewer than one in five animals requires treatment each year (and many of these are routine preventive measures or repeat treatments for the same pathology). Zoo animals customarily live far, far longer than animals in nature.

I like to remind you that Emil, as a very human being, represents you, and that the animals are part of your family. So I hope that when you look at these pictures you will pay special attention to the emotions involved, particularly your own. If that strikes you as being too serious, just look at the pictures and have fun.

Monday

It is not unusual for the week to start with a bang. Emil is away from the zoo over weekends unless there has been an emergency or unless he's on administrative duty. The keepers have had an additional two days to observe their charges; Saturday's minor ailments may be quite demanding by Monday, and the two days of heaviest public attendance have just passed.

True to form, this Monday has a problem waiting for Emil when he gets in at about 8:30 A.M. Two Talipoin monkeys have arrived, both very weak, a newborn and a pregnant female ready to deliver but not yet in labor. The story is that the female has been in labor but has stopped. The newborn monkey was being carried around by another female which had also been pregnant. Which female does the newborn belong to? Does this female have a fetus it can't deliver? Examination readily discloses that the monkey has not yet produced a baby, and that she has a fetus ready to deliver but no uterine contractions to power the delivery. The baby monkey is put in the incubator, and given a rolled-up towel to cling to. Joe then prepares the pregnant female for a Caesarean section while Emil and Gráinne scrub. What a way to start a week!

Joe tapes the monkey into position on the operating table. (The towel draping the table seems to have been put in the sterilizer as a gag. Its inscription reads: "It's your move, tiger.") The operation consists of making a midline incision in the abdominal wall, bringing the uterus up into the operative field, and making an incision in the fundus of the uterus through which the fetus is delivered. Despite the small size of the patient, the team works smoothly and del-

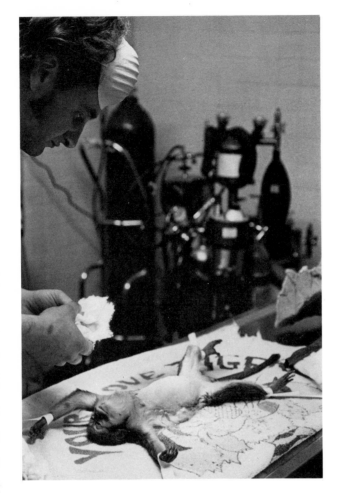

icately. Everything clicks along beautifully, and the operation is over in twenty minutes. While Emil and Gráinne get out of their gowns, Joe cleans and dries the new baby and puts it in the incubator, where in the meantime the first baby monkey, still grasping the folded towel, has died.

The operation is so handily performed that it has a certain ballet-like quality that is very satisfying. Words cannot convey the excitement, the thrill, and the grandeur of the moment the fetus is lifted from the womb. He looks so ancient! It seems as if thousands of years of racial history had been graven into that tiny body. A minute later he is just a cute newborn monkey, but for that initial moment he is invested with a primordial dignity.

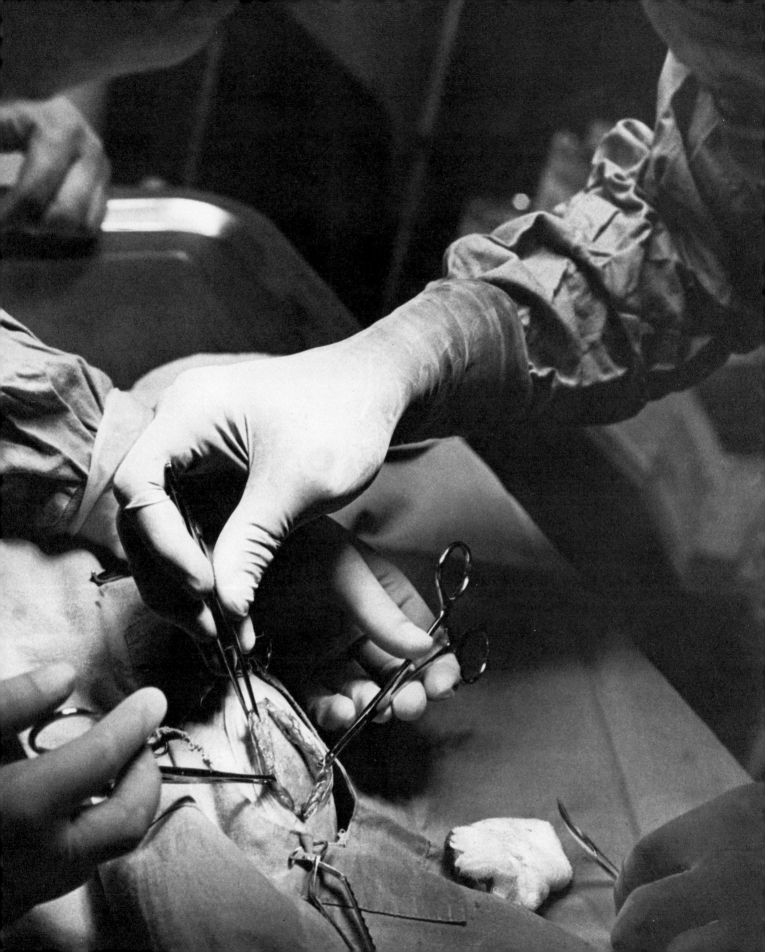

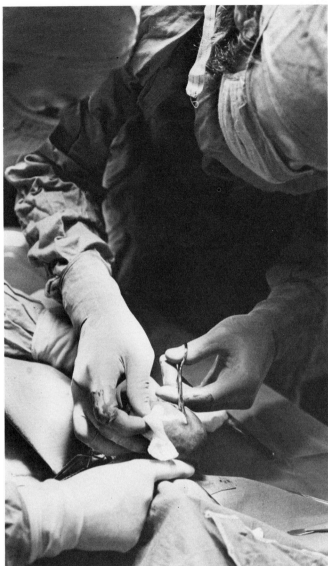

First Emil makes the abdominal incision. He usually operates with a quality of intensity that seems to create a visual tube locking him in with his patient. The next step is the incision in the uterus itself.

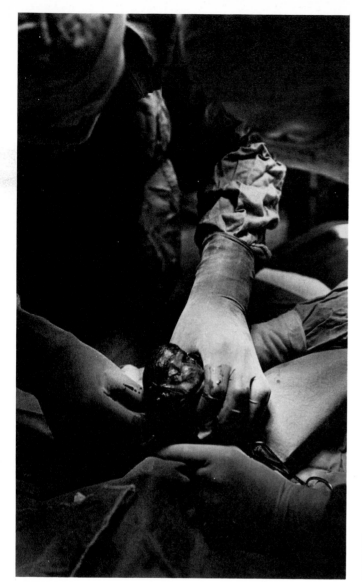

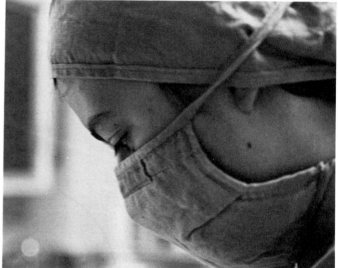

The head appears in the uterine
incision and is then eased out.
Gráinne is momentarily breathless at
the dramatic climax of the operation
as the fetus is delivered.

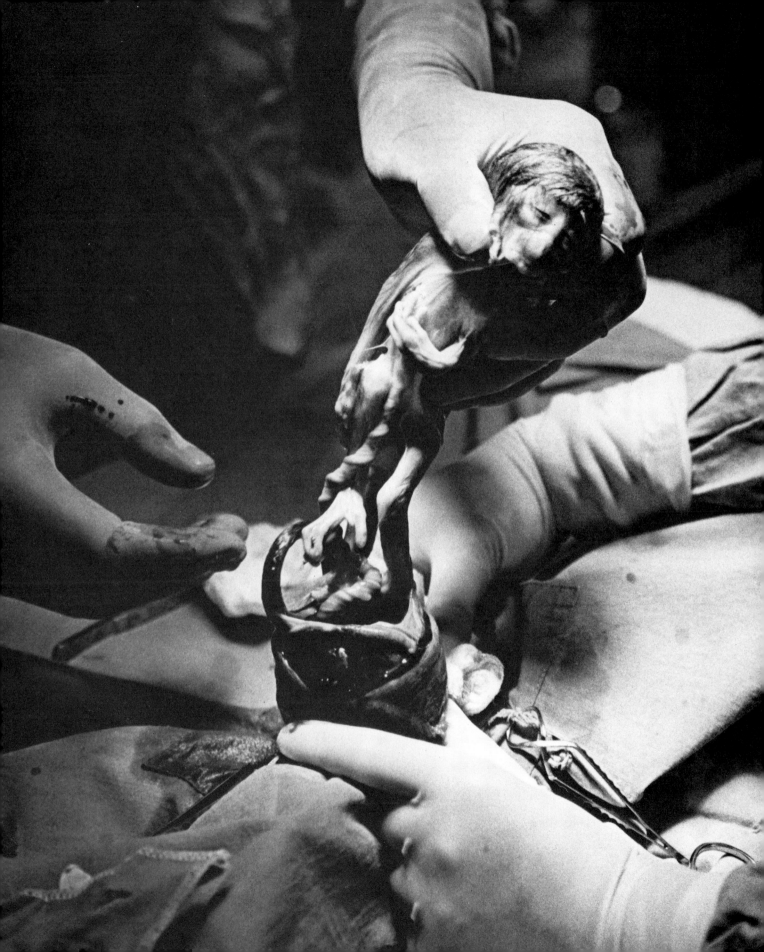

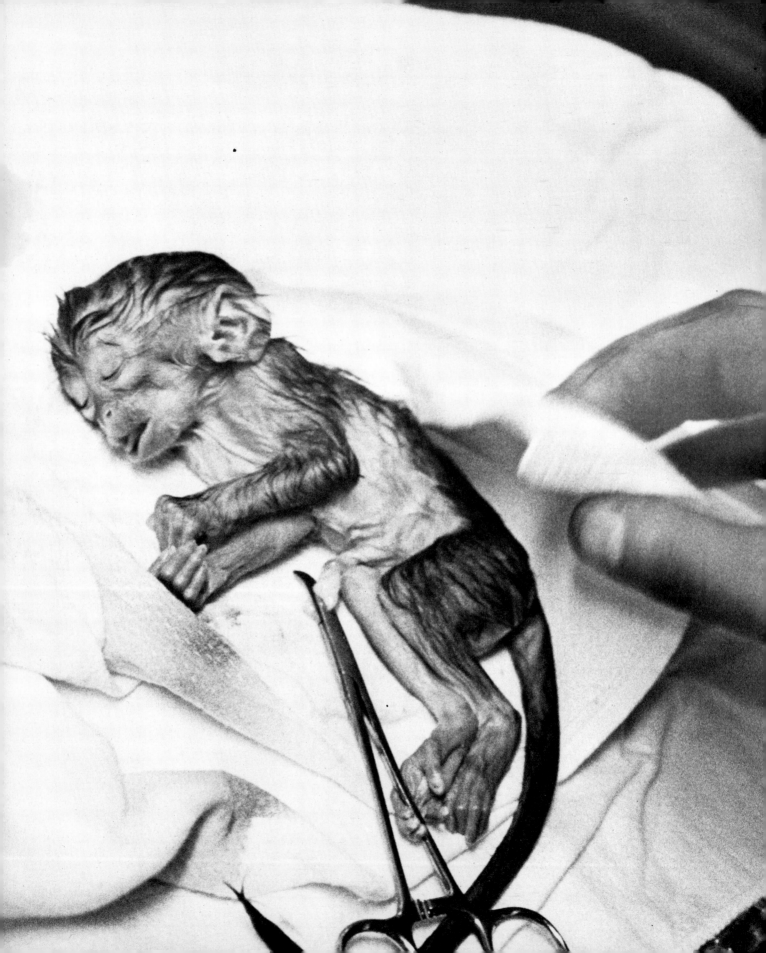

*Joe tenderly cleans the baby, paying
special attention to clearing the
airway. Even after a brief operation
that has gone smoothly, Emil shows
the strain of his intense concentration.*

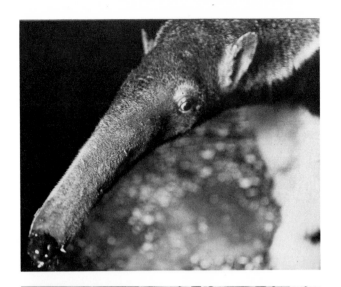

After checking the reports on his desk, Emil sets out on his daily rounds. One of the highlights of the morning is a visit to a young giant anteater. Since he is an anteater, his chief instrument of relationship is his nose. He will often raise a forefoot with its imposing hook-like claw in a tentative grasping gesture which one usually avoids with care. A few months after this picture was taken, the anteater used his formidable claws to dig out from under his enclosure and ended up in a pen with some peccaries, who viciously attacked and mauled him. When I visited him in the hospital shortly after that, he was lying on his side in some straw and breathing with difficulty, his eyes closed. As I approached, he opened his expressive eyes, struggled painfully to his feet, and shambled toward the front of the hospital cage, his nose eagerly presented for greeting. Halfway there he staggered, keeled over on his side, and lay there panting, looking up with a clear appeal. It was heartbreaking. He died a few hours later.

Emil continues his ride through the park, eyeing the occupants as he slowly passes each compound, occasionally stopping to get reports or exchange observations with the keepers. The next stop is a pause to admire the aoudads, beautiful and nimble mountain or Barbary sheep. This is Grandpa Aoudad, the dignity and gravity of his years pictured in his magnificent head.

If there is one area of the park that could be considered Emil's favorite, it's the South American Plains exhibit. Hardly a day goes by that he doesn't spend at least a couple of minutes in this verdant field. Today Emil is attracted by a baby guanaco. Guanacos look much like llamas, but they have never been domesticated. Emil pets the baby guanaco while Susie supervises. Guanacos are naturally curious, but Susie is an unusual character. She takes it upon herself to be the hostess of the South American Plains and presents herself for petting to all visitors, closely accompanying them throughout their visit.

The Formosan
sika deer are in
a large wooded
area. They too
are curious, but
at a distance. A
keeper has
reported
noticing a lump
over the eye of
one of the herd,
and Emil stops
to take a look.

Having located the deer with the tumor, Emil injects him with a tranquilizer and takes him to the hospital. Emil removes the tumor, takes the deer back to the compound, and injects him with an antidote to the tranquilizer. The antidote takes effect rapidly and suddenly, so that Joe, who has been holding the animal in position for the injection, is taken by surprise when the deer quickly leaps up.

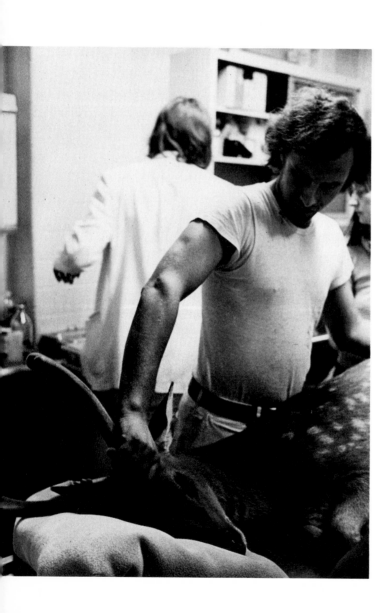

The final stop on today's rounds is at the Reptile House. Everything about this area is different. Snakes are somehow stranger than the other beasts. Their biology is different, their emotional responses seem greatly limited and harder (or impossible) to read, and they are in general the most dangerous group to handle. Snakes are rarely brought to the hospital. In the Reptile House there are "sick rooms" for those which are ill and for the quarantine of new arrivals. When a snake needs medical attention, it is not handled by the hospital attendants, but by the snake keepers. One gets the impression that the snake keepers allow Emil near their charges only out of unavoidable necessity, with some misgivings, and only when they say it's all right for him to approach. The snake keepers are different too. The strangeness of their animals, and, perhaps even more, the danger of their work impart to them a certain clear mystique. They live in an atmosphere of syringes with antivenin, of alarm gongs, of warning gongs, of emergency telephone systems. The doors on the rear of the snake enclosures are carefully constructed, carefully stenciled with warning signs; the spitting cobra's cage has a face mask at the bottom of the door. Behind the cages and in the various handling areas emergency telephones are stationed. The ominous signs make visitors nervous, but to the snake men it's just part of

the familiar daily scenery. When they handle the snakes, they must be at the peak of alertness, with instantaneous reflexes prepared to operate at any moment. They must be completely familiar with the tools of their craft and must have a thorough knowledge of each species they're responsible for. It's a formidable job.

Some people are repelled by snakes, some are fascinated by them, but very few are totally indifferent. I don't know why snakes have the quality of arousing strong emotions in man. There are those who are inexplicably terrified by even nonpoisonous snakes. Snakes are not "slimy," and some are quite agreeable to handle. But they're hardly responsive, and not much good for romping with.

A salesman once came into the hospital to convince Emil to order his brand of supplies. He was so insistent and so inconsiderate of Emil's pressures and limited time that, after a long while, Emil was forced to walk away. The salesman promptly went into the tissue pathology lab and continued his spiel, interrupting Carlos's work. Emil walked into the lab and, without saying a word, bent down and started looking under the counters. After a minute or two Carlos asked him what in hell he was doing. In a strained voice Emil replied: "A Russell's viper got out of his bag." Carlos promptly got down to join the search. When they looked up, the salesman was gone.

On the left is Pete. He's an outstanding authority on Crocodilia, but here he's holding a small scrub python. And on the right is Bob holding an Indian python.

Some of the snakes are tiny and some
are huge, but size is no gauge of their
dangerousness. On the left, below, is a
red-tailed rat snake, which has a rash.
On the right is a boa constrictor. His
size is imposing, but he is as harmless
as the rat snake.

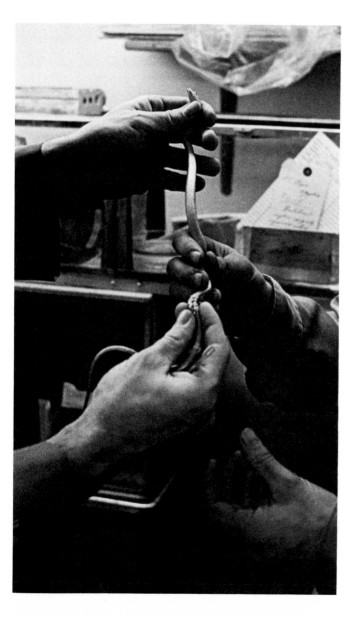

Below, Emil is looking into the throat of an Indian python. I can't imagine where a snake's throat ends, but for practical purposes I suppose it goes down as far as the flashlight can illuminate. On the right, medication is being injected into the stomach of a blood python with an intestinal problem.

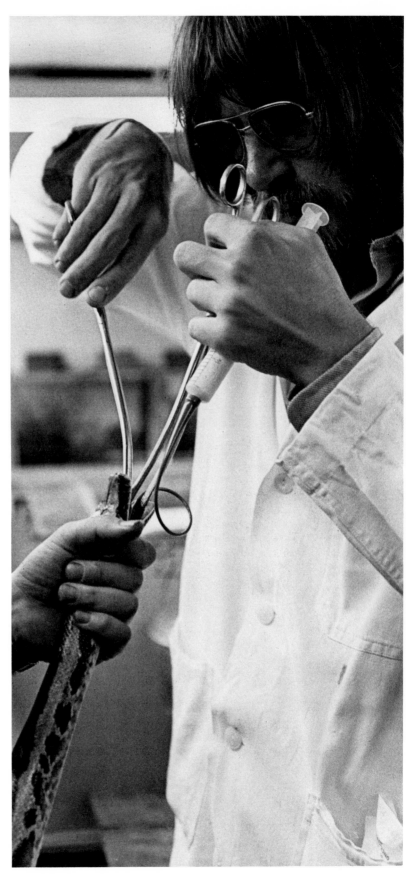

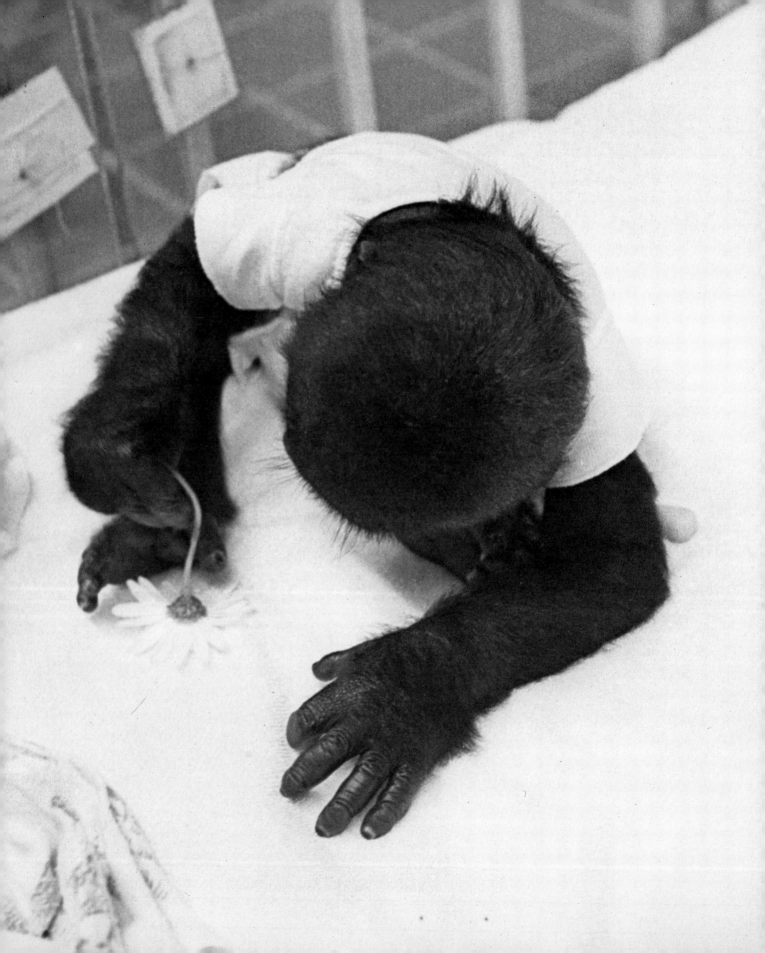

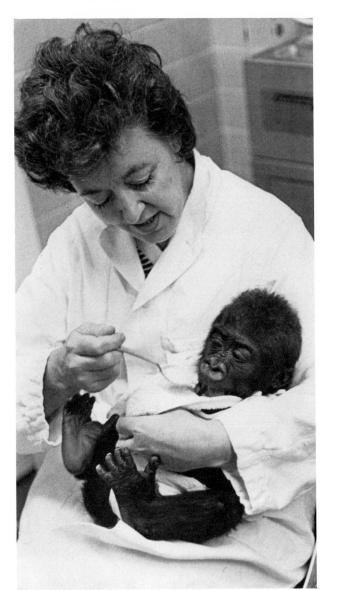

Emil is very late for lunch today and tarries awhile before returning to his remaining chores. It isn't because of fatigue—although it has been a very full day indeed—but rather some slight reluctance to face a quantity of paper work which, though very important, is rarely very exciting. The paper work done, Emil ends his day on a cheerful note. He stops at the hospital nursery to visit and examine Patty-cake, who is living there with her surrogate mother, Caroline Atkinson. Patty-cake, you may remember, is the baby gorilla from the Central Park Zoo who got caught in an altercation between her mother and her father and ended up with a broken arm. It was felt she could be cared for best by Emil at his hospital, and she was duly sent there to recuperate. When these pictures were made, she was four months old and her arm was healed. She had also been a little malnourished, but her nutrition was readily improved.

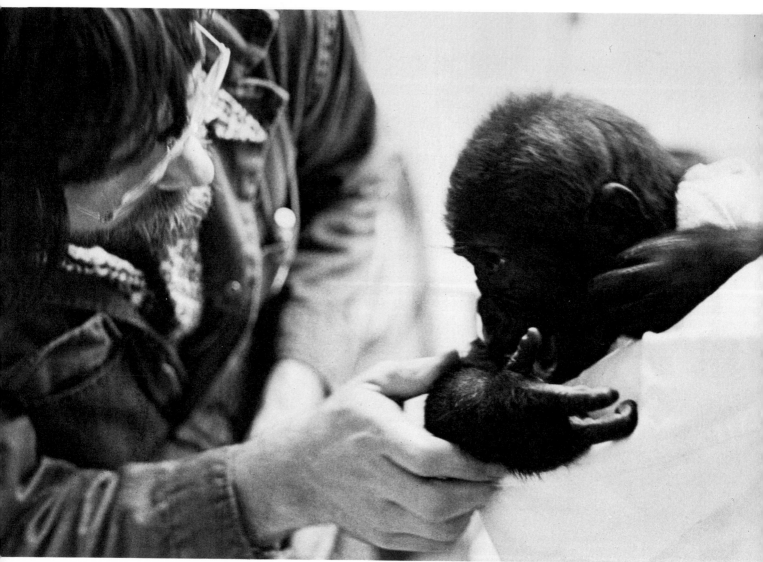

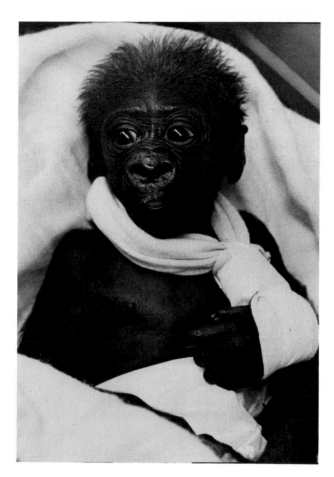

Caroline stayed with Patty-cake day and night, caring for her just as she would a human baby. Indeed the nursery looked like any other, with its playpen, baby toys, cans of Enfamil, and boxes of Pampers. Patty-cake herself was most engaging, obviously very much attached to Caroline and curious about her environment. She played (but not for long) with anything that came her way, ate her baby food, submitted to having her diapers changed, and slept a good deal. On warm sunny afternoons she was taken to a special section of the Lowland Gorilla exhibit, where she sat in the sun with Caroline and some toys.

Patty-cake's story is not strikingly unusual. Baby gorillas are no longer rarities in good zoos. And incidents of child abuse are not infrequent among gorillas. Not long after Patty-cake's return to the Central Park Zoo, a baby gorilla at the Bronx Zoo turned up with a shattered elbow, possibly the result of having been thrown across the cage by his father. In the hospital the baby was named Joe Willie in honor of Joe Namath, who was in another hospital with a similar injury (not from a similar cause). Emil puts Joe Willie's arm in a sling after treating him with the help of a pediatric orthopedist. The arm healed well, and he regained full motion.

Tuesday

As you can see, the animals are handled with practiced skill and confidence. Although most animals rarely require medical attention, some, such as the elephant, the rhinoceros, the alligator, almost never need treatment. When they do, the approach may be more tentative and exploratory. Several such occasions have arisen this week, and it must be said that an outsider might be reminded at times of a Marx Brothers' comedy. This Tuesday morning a keeper calls in and reports that one of the large alligators seems lame, that he seems to be favoring his right front paw. Usually when an animal is reported lame, Emil and Joe hop into the ambulance, help the keeper corral the patient, and Emil does a quick field examination. Not so this time. Rationalizing that the animal would surely need an X-ray, Emil tells the keeper to catch the alligator and put him in the ambulance which they will send over. One can only guess at the expression on the keeper's face.

After a long period that must have been filled with untold adventures, the keeper arrives at the hospital with his charge safely ensconced in the ambulance. The keeper's face isn't hard to read, but it's difficult to make out how the alligator felt about it.

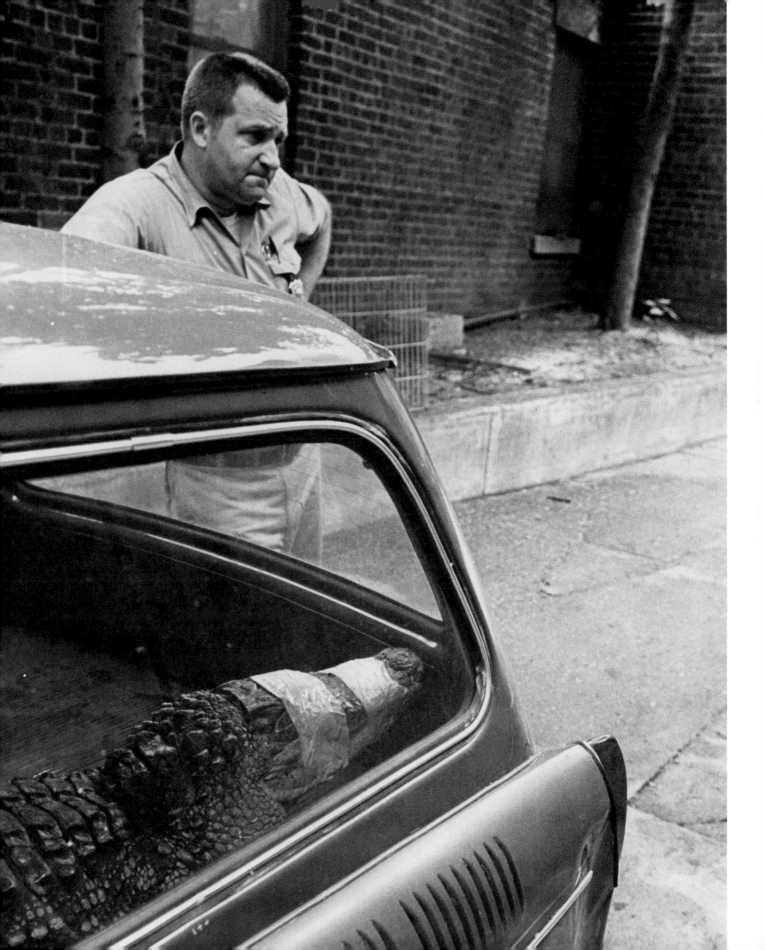

Usually a new arrival galvanizes the hospital staff into immediate, effective, coordinated action. In this instance it is a few minutes before Jim saunters out to evaluate the situation. After a while Emil and Joe join the party, probably hoping that by the time they arrive the keeper and Jim will have the alligator well in hand. No such luck. Instead of the usual bustling efficiency, there follows a period of quiet contemplation. They contemplate the sky, they contemplate each other, and finally they contemplate the alligator. The alligator contemplates them right back.

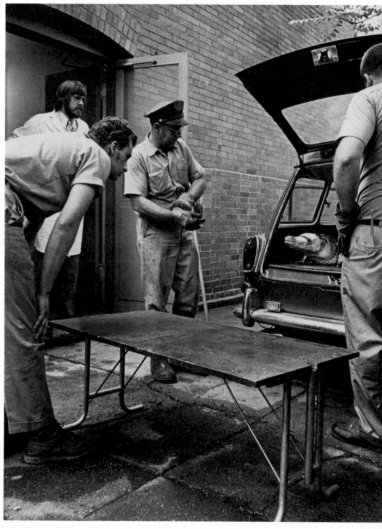

They decide to put the alligator on the table, strap him in place, and wheel him into the X-ray room to have his picture taken. It is voted that the keeper will take the head. While Emil and Joe strap the animal down, the keeper holds him in place. Despite the success of the undertaking up to this point, it is clear that the keeper has gained neither confidence nor satisfaction from the procedure.

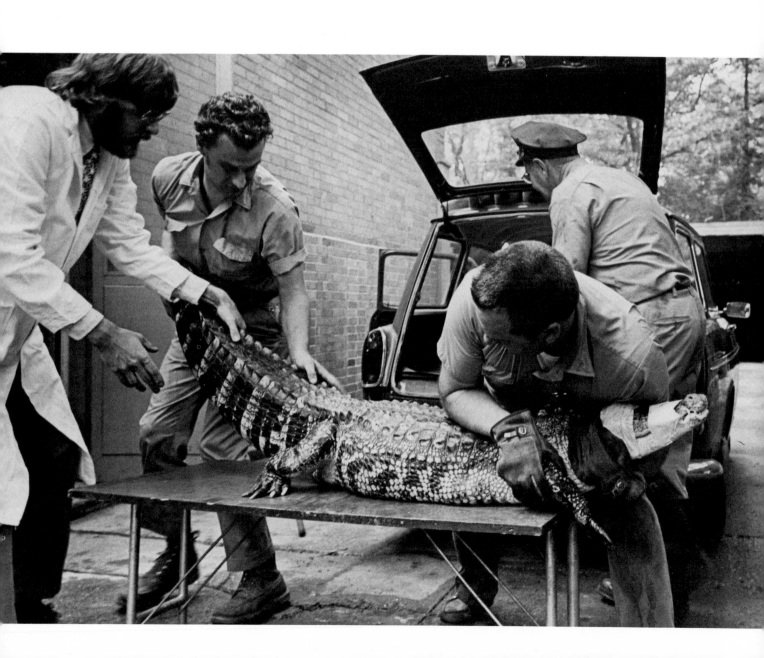

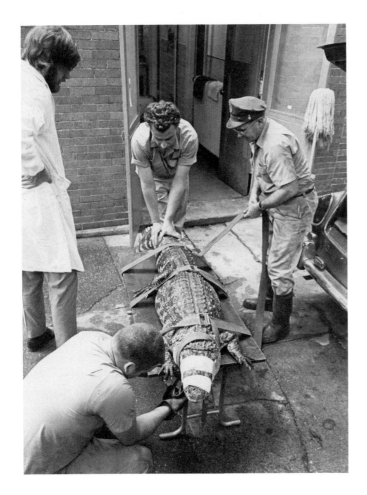

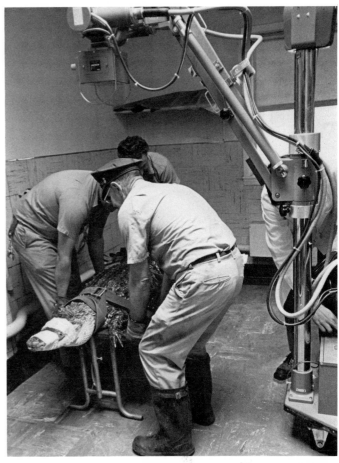

At this point several of the people look a little smug, but the alligator looks as if he were having fantasies of revenge. Taking the X-ray seems almost an anticlimax after all this activity. In the darkroom Emil is once again the poised and confident scientist —master of himself and his domain. The X-ray shows no abnormality. There isn't much wrong with the alligator's foot.

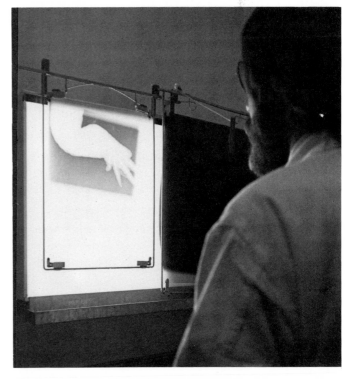

After this incident Emil immediately gets into the ambulance and heads for the South American Plains. He explains that he's going in such a hurry because he is eager to inject some antibiotic into a tapir with a staphylococcus infection. But as soon as he gets to the field, he sits down on a rock and proceeds to absorb the serenity of the surroundings while Jim Doherty, the Assistant Curator of Mammals, tries to lure the sick tapir out of a pond. While Emil is waiting, another tapir quietly approaches him from behind and then suddenly pokes with his nose. One cannot always be sure of a tapir's temperament, but these on the Plains are consistently placid and friendly, and sometimes, as you see, they even try to be cute. One never walks unescorted in this area. Good hosts that they are, the animals even conduct departing visitors to the gate.

A while ago the zoo was receiving a shipment of tapirs for the South American Plains. The truck backed up to the gate, a ramp was set up, and the animals duly walked down the ramp into the Plains. All except the last one, who got down, walked around the truck, and started on a voyage of exploration. Startled by this rugged individualism, the crew gawked for a moment and then took off lickety-split to catch up with her. But despite their clumsy appearance tapirs can run pretty fast. Emil, who has a much better build for running, couldn't catch her. Since she allowed him within a certain distance, he decided to lasso her, which he succeeded in doing. But the tapir's figure that didn't hamper her running did hamper the roping. She slid right out of it and took off again.

No one ever mentioned how the zoo visitors reacted to the sight of a tapir

streaking down the road followed by a long-legged doctor with his white coat flapping in the breeze and a lasso whirling around his head. The crew again got within reasonable distance of her and tried to herd her up against a walk. She simply stared at them and charged through the line. By this time she'd gotten pretty near the gates, and they had to order the park entrances and exits closed. They really didn't want her wandering around the Bronx. Finally somebody got the idea of confronting her with an open crate. One was quickly procured and, much to everyone's surprise, she walked right in.

*Fortunately most tapirs stay at home
and lie around and dunk in the pond
and, sometimes, have babies.*

Emil next has some birds to look at. The tiny rhea chick on the left has a salmonella infection. Rheas are ostrich-like birds weighing around eighty pounds. They are generally peaceful but can get ornery. The frogmouth is quite another matter. These birds seem to like people pretty well. Their direct, owl-like stare is engaging, and their feathers are so arranged as to give them a distinctly fuzzy appearance. These Australian birds look like owls, but they are not even closely related.

This strange-looking creature glaring at you is a cassowary, and his character is written all over his face. A while ago this gigantic bird took a dislike to one particular keeper, as animals will occasionally do. One day when the disliked keeper came down the narrow passageway between the cages, this cassowary lay in wait for him. As he passed the bird's enclosure she hauled off with such a mighty kick at the iron caging that its front wall tore loose from the concrete in which its large pins were embedded. The keeper got out of the way in time and the cage wall was replaced, but there's still a large dent from the kick mark in the heavy iron sheet at its base. From the bird exhibits Emil makes a quick check on the siamangs, who prove to be in good condition. You'd never think so to listen to them. These relatives of the gibbon have a muscular pouch under the skin of their throats. They fill the pouch with air through a hole in the trachea and then force it back in, making an unbearably loud, bloodcurdling noise. The fellow in the picture is about to perform. Siamangs are one of the few monogamous primates, but that probably doesn't account for the noise.

The next stop is a visit to a beautiful Thompson's gazelle who seems to be having trouble with her vision. She is

ordered into the hospital to await examination by Dr. Roy Bellhorn, the ophthalmologist. It was subsequently determined that she was totally blind and that her blindness was irreversible. In her cage in the hospital she managed quite well by virtue of an extraordinary sense of hearing and, one would guess, her sense of smell. No matter how quietly a visitor approached she would promptly come to the front of the cage, to the exact spot where the visitor was standing, and present her nose to be patted. The problem in such instances is one of disposition. What does one do with a blind gazelle? A lot of buying, selling, and trading goes on between zoos and animal compounds throughout the world, but a disabled animal is, of course, out of the market. The gazelle was on many people's minds for quite a while. She couldn't go back to the compound because she couldn't compete for food and, more important, she'd get in trouble with the ostriches who were in the same area. The final plan was heartwarming indeed. She would be put in a rather small, clear, open area and left there alone until she learned the boundaries and the terrain. This area would then be used to receive and introduce new animals of related species into the park. The blind "Tommy" would be the official hostess, and her job would be to greet the new animals and help them get acclimated.

On to the larger animals. Emil checks the zoo's yak herd, which is in great shape and quite productive, as the youngsters in the picture attest.

Next is a quick visit with the friendly takin, which is easily persuaded to haul his ponderous self onto his hind legs to greet Emil. These exceedingly rare animals, which look a little like musk oxen, are surprisingly fast and agile despite their bulk. As a matter of fact, until one learns better one is frequently surprised at the speed and nimbleness of many wild animals which seem massive or clumsy or dull.

Nearby are the polar bears, in various attitudes of repose. It is a warm day and they are enjoying the comfort of their cool shower which a keeper has thoughtfully set up for them. The next problem concerns a couple of lesser pandas which are residing in a nice big cage they have come to regard as home. The fellow above is curled up on a wooden ledge making it clear that he is quite comfortable there. The relocation authorities have, however, ruled otherwise. A very fine, very large, very woodsy environment has been constructed for the lesser pandas where they will be completely uncaged, separated from the public only by a relatively low concrete wall. Lots of soil, bushes, brush, trees to climb, rocks, and a tiny stream. But they aren't going to move voluntarily.

Out come the nets and up go the pandas.
Visitors gather around to watch the
show. A very large lady grumbles,
"Why are they harassing that cute
fuzzy-wuzzy?" Emil watches tensely,
knowing that although lesser pandas
are climbing animals they tend to be
clumsy, and one of them might well
fall and hurt himself.

Once in their new home, the animals
spend some time running around and
exploring the area. The fellow who
was disturbed when curled up on
the wooden ledge in the old cage
resumes his position here, this time
surrounded by all the furnishings of
panda luxury.

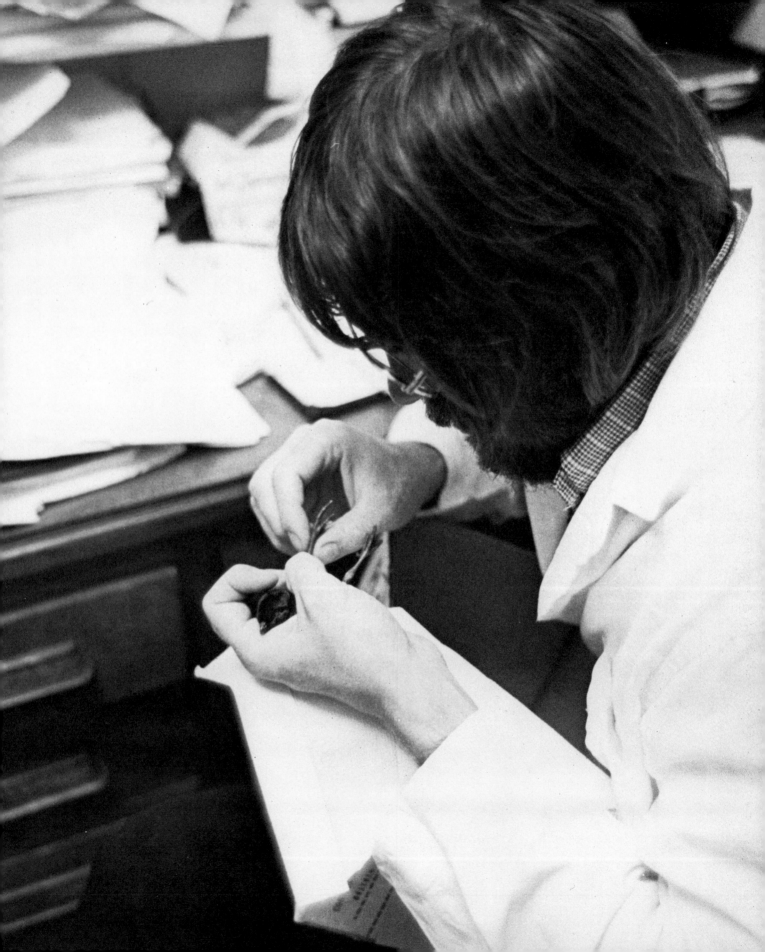

It has been another full morning, and Emil is glad for a lunch break. He still has the hospital patients to check, and he knows there is a long day ahead. Someone has brought, in a cardboard box, a baby crested wood partirdge, which seems to have some trouble with one of its legs. Emil checks it over and finds no injuries.

Someone has also brought, in a much larger box, a young orangutan for the zoo's collection. She must spend some time in quarantine, and Jim has given her a blanket, which she holds spread out over her head, covering herself and then cautiously opening the folds to look at the people outside the cage. Later on, she comes to the front of the cage and ends up by kissing Joe's face. He is so thrilled that he runs from room to room in the hospital, announcing excitedly to the occupants, "She kissed me! She kissed me!" Carlos looks up from his microtome and says, "Ask her if she's got a friend for me."

In an isolation cage is a beautiful clouded leopard with a virus disease called rhino-tracheitis. This illness is highly infectious among felines, and its appearance calls for stringent measures to prevent an epidemic. Note the clouded eyes.

The subject of felines brings to mind a young mountain lion who had been quarantined in the hospital for some time before being sent out to be placed on exhibit. Every young feline that is in the hospital for any length of time becomes a pet, and Carlos was no exception. Everybody played with him, and his cage was occasionally left bolted but unlocked. After a while he somehow learned to open the bolt (Joe was suspected of patiently drilling him) so that he could, and sometimes did, go for an unscheduled walk through the hospital. Shortly after Carlos was transferred out of the hospital, a keeper neglected to lock his cage in the building where he was then housed. In a short while a couple of startled keepers came upon a six-month-old mountain lion strolling about the building. They locked some doors, signaled an emergency, and consulted. The cat was much too big to be netted, and the keepers, now joined by all the staff in the area, weren't about to try to herd him in and risk his getting panicky—his teeth and claws were much too imposing for that. Finally they called Emil and asked him to come over and shoot the animal with his CO_2 pistol Emil came over, opened the door to the area in which Carlos had been confined, called him over, picked him up, and deposited him in his cage. Emil walked right out, dead-pan, without saying a word to six crestfallen keepers gathered in the doorway.

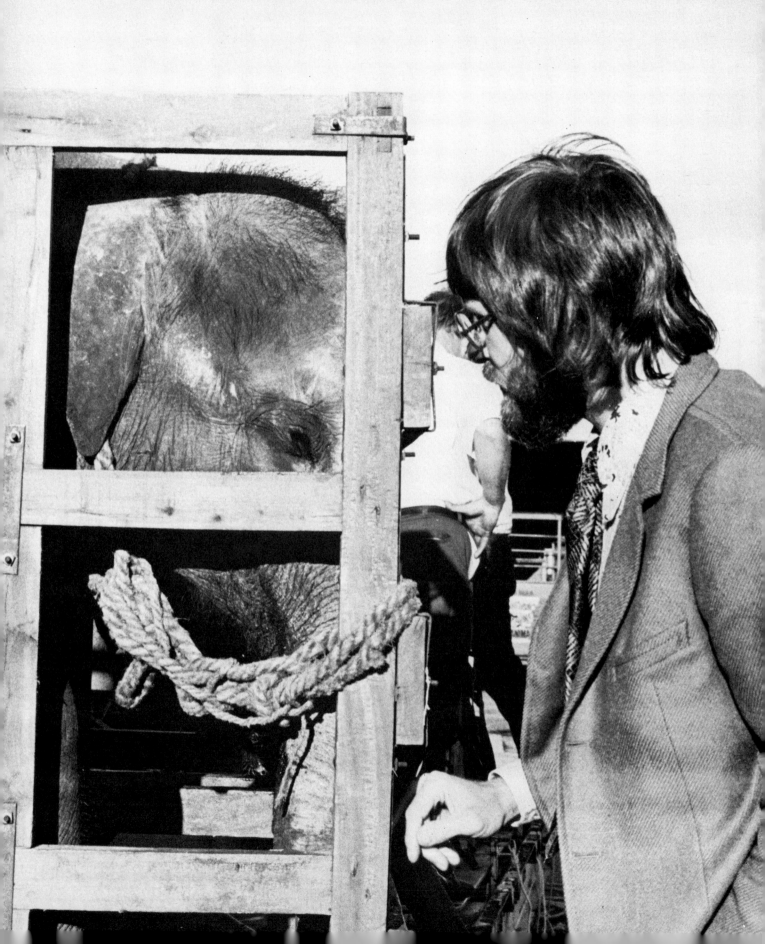

One would think that this had already been a long day. It is, however, destined to be a long day's journey into night. Four baby elephants are due to arrive at the airport at 6:00 P.M. The zoo has begun work on an Asian Plains exhibit, and this is to

be, when completed, the elephants' ultimate home. Off to the airport goes Emil to see what shape they have arrived in. It appears that they have arrived in the shape of four crates on a rolling platform. They are about four feet high at the shoulder, munch continuously on sugar cane, and are as friendly as the crates allow them to be.

Emil gives the official greeting and, looking them over, decides that they not only look well but are very cute indeed. Dr. Alan Belson, Emil's assistant, watches as the crates are pushed into the ASPCA shelter at the airport. It requires some hours to get the various papers signed and the red tape untangled at the airport. The crates are then loaded onto a truck and carefully and slowly driven to the zoo. By the time they arrive, it is after midnight and pitch black except for the area in front of the elephant house lighted by a group of jerry-rigged floodlights. Milling about the area are perhaps a dozen keepers, with the ubiquitous Jim Doherty and Joe Ruf checking the preparations. There is something of a party-like atmosphere as the group waits for the truck, joking and clowning, telling stories, and speculating about the baby elephants.

As soon as the truck arrives, Jim Doherty and Joe Ruf organize a group of keepers to get the first crate down on the ground and over into the pen. The other crates soon follow. Before the crates are opened, Emil, with Gráinne's help, draws some blood from the elephants' ear veins. The idea is that, in the crates, the little fellows' movements will be restricted. But they have been in those crates long enough to learn how to squeeze the last inch of movement out of the available space. It seems as though the babies were in constant motion. Getting a needle in a vein proves to be an acrobatic feat, but Emil finally manages to get the job done.

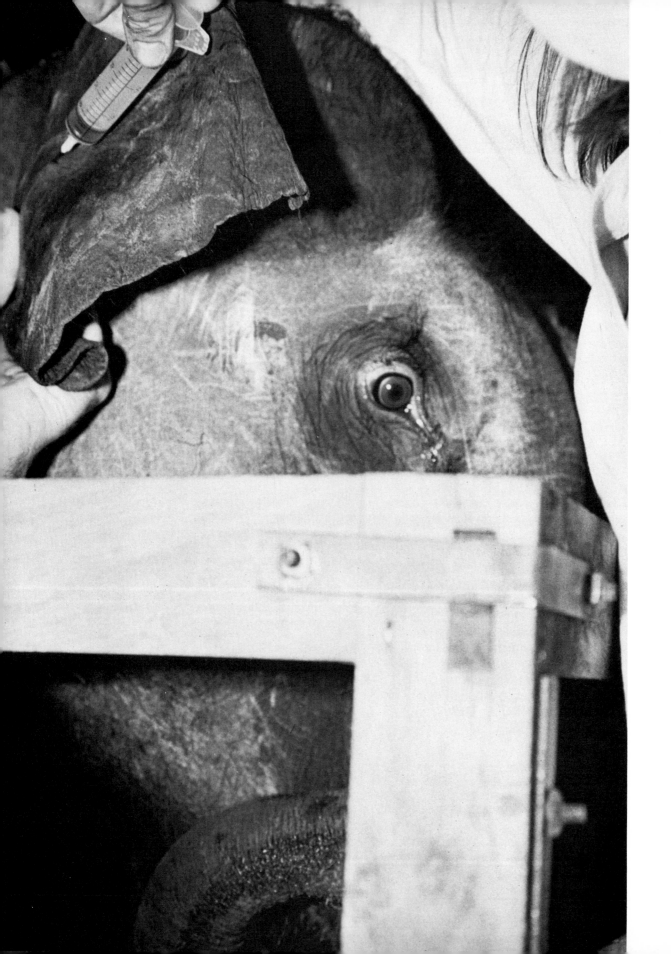

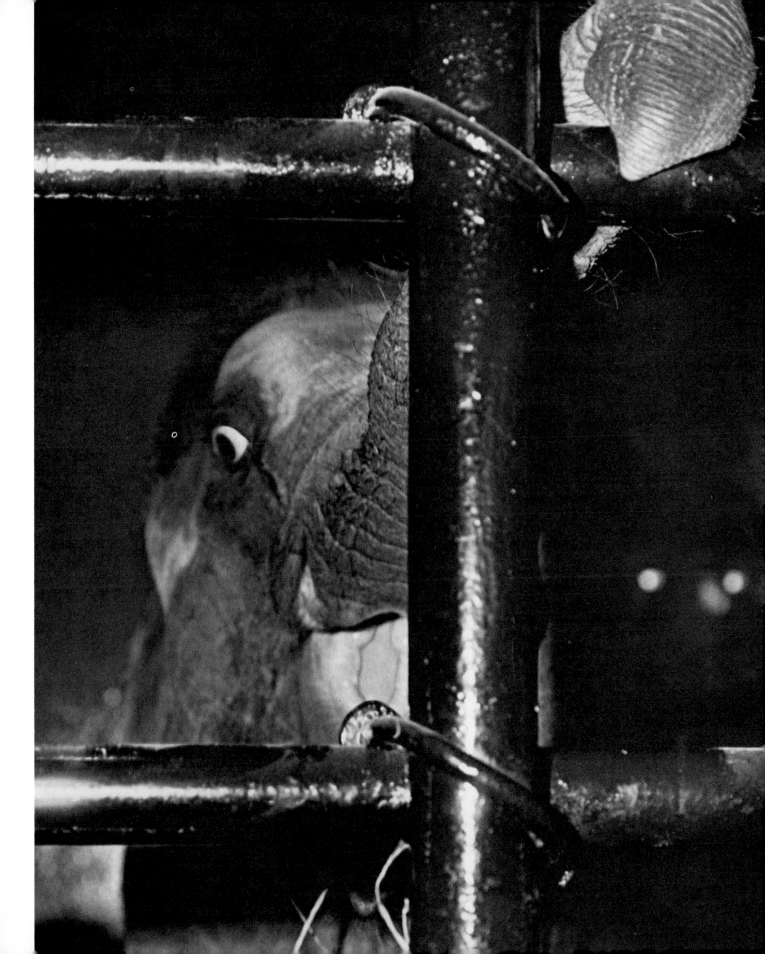

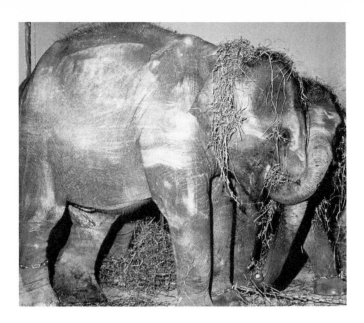

Once out of the crates the babies are clearly happy. They don't exactly scamper about, but they do shuffle mightily. They play with the straw on the floor, explore the bars on the front of the enclosure, and do a good deal of shrill trumpeting. One can't tell whether it is high spirits, fraternal concern, or just plain confusion that makes this little fellow keep putting hay in the wrong mouths. He later showed himself to be a little devil, constantly playing tricks on the others. Some people claimed they could see a mischievous glint in his eye that very first night.

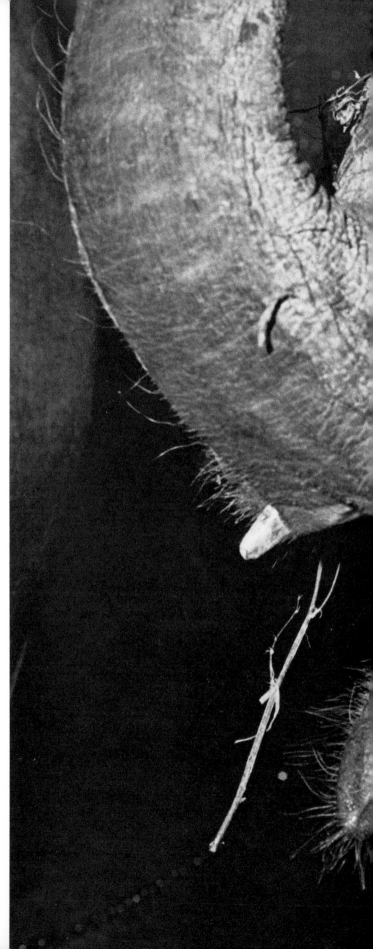

Wednesday

This morning is spent at the Aquarium, which is also Emil's responsibility, although it's usually delegated to Dr. Jay Hyman, the Zoological Society's specialist in aquatic mammals. On special occasions, however, Emil checks things out himself, and this is a special occasion. The keepers at the Aquarium noticed that Francis, a Beluga whale, was off her feed, that she had a mucous discharge, and that her breasts were protruding a bit. Bill Flynn, Curator of the Aquarium, felt there was a chance she might be pregnant. Emil and Jay decided they would examine Francis, take some blood for hormone studies, and get someone with an electronic stethoscope to listen for fetal heart sounds. The ordinary pregnancy tests used for human beings don't seem to work for whales.

Anything one does with a whale, beyond just looking at it, is a project. Everybody begins the morning by looking at Francis. After a period of looking, the consensus is that Francis looks a bit seedy. The first step in the procedure is to drain the pool, which is divided into a large, shallow section, and a smaller section about three feet deeper. When the pool is drained to the level of the deep area, a large section of its floor is available to personnel and Francis is confined to the adjoining deeper section. She is maneuvered onto a stretcher which is brought over to the dry section of the floor. The doctors, in wet-suits or waders, can then work with her while the keepers hold the stretcher in place. Having directed the procedure thus far, Bill Flynn devotes himself to holding the whale's head, patting her, and being generally soothing.

100

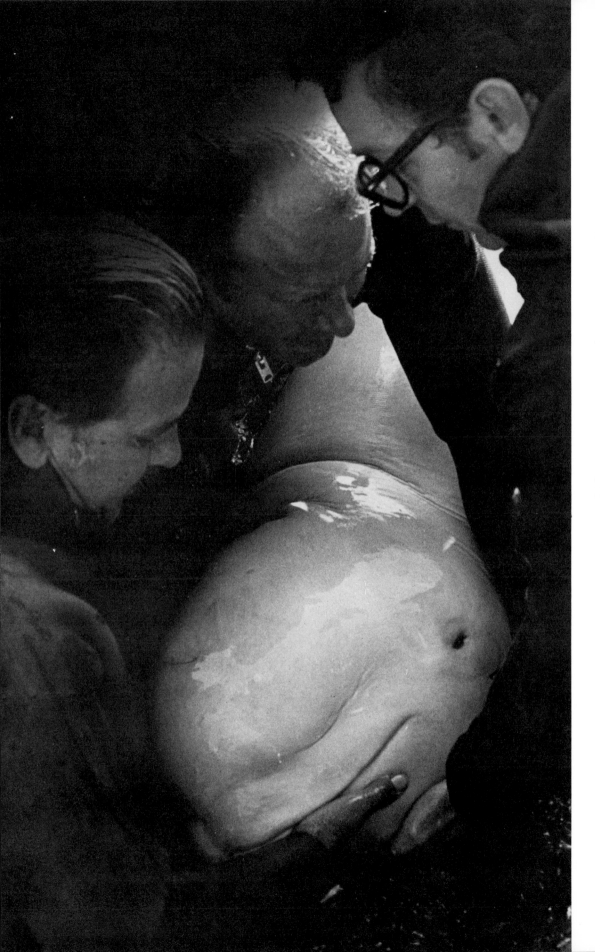

Here is Francis
with Bill Flynn,
at the far right,
holding her head.
The New York
Times *in an
article about
Francis made
special note of
her "Mona Lisa
smile." Francis is
known as
"Francis" rather
than "Frances,"
incidentally,
because she was
named for the
Indian who caught
her.*

Emil and a keeper sit for a while at the edge of the pool to observe Francis more closely. She seems to be her usual friendly self as she sails over to greet them.
The water level is lowered so that Francis is somewhat confined. The keepers assemble the stretcher while Emil looks on. Francis, who seems to know from past experience what is going on, withdraws to the farthest corner of the pool.

The stretcher is brought into the water. A group of keepers range alongside one pole of the stretcher while Bill and some of the other men maneuver Francis onto the stretcher, which is then propelled over to the dry area, where the front ends of the stretcher poles are rested on the concrete ledge.

Dr. Walter Feder, from Maimonides Hospital, listens through an electronically amplified stethoscope to identify fetal heart sounds. Above the pool this machine translates the amplified sounds into motion which is recorded on a long strip of paper, much like an electrocardiograph tracing. Down below one can see through the glassed guardrail Dr. Feder and the crew working on the whale.

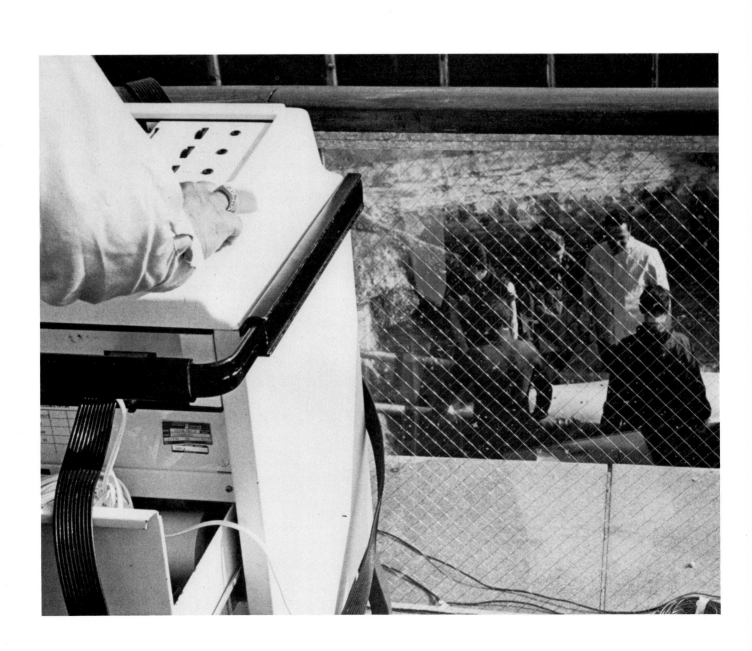

Dr. Hyman, having decided that, pregnant or not, Francis probably has a low-grade systemic infection, injects an antibiotic while Bill continues his patting and soothing. Infection? Probably. Pregnancy? Undecided. Jay decides to do a pelvic examination. On the right is the portrait of a specialist in aquatic mammals doing a pelvic exam on a whale named Francis.

There is an unhappy conclusion to the story of Francis. It turned out that she was indeed pregnant. Some months after these photographs were made, she seemed ready to deliver, but the fetus died and Francis did not expel it. She developed a severe toxemia, and, with the fetus still in utero, she herself died. To those who had worked with her during the long, uncertain course of her pregnancy, the end was a devastating emotional experience. Many people in the area who followed the news of her condition with interest and sympathy will long remember this endearing creature.

The morning ends with the issue of pregnancy unresolved. After lunch Emil returns to the zoo to crowd a full day's work into a long afternoon. First on the agenda is a black wolf which has been reported ailing. The procedure is to herd the wolf into the smallest pen available so that Emil can inject a tranquilizer with the CO_2 pistol. Well, if that wolf is ailing he must be something to see in action when he's in good shape! He is just too quick and too agile for Emil to get a shot at him. Emil might succeed if he had all afternoon to wear the wolf down, but this is a busy day. Emil needs to get a shot at the wolf's rear end, but that wolf does a lot of fast moving around, never presenting Emil with anything other than his head with its gleaming eyes and bared fangs. (This was the only time during the making of this book that Emil failed with the pistol, though he did manage to tranquilize the wolf the following day.)

On his way to see a mandrill Emil
stops for a moment to commune with
the hippos. Although they rarely have
any medical problems, the large
animals are visited regularly. Emil
makes a point of patting one, talking
to another, giving an apple to a
third. As Emil says, "In case
something does go wrong with one of
them I want them to know me and
think kindly of me."

The mandrill doesn't think kindly of anyone. He doesn't know Emil and doesn't want to. He has a bad infection in his heel. His usually nasty disposition has become worse, and he has retired to a corner of his cage, sitting there glumly glowering at the world. When mealtimes arrive he refuses to stir, and has the females bring food to him. He is in a mean mood, and there is no thought of walking up to him and giving him an injection. Since he is big and powerful, he can't be netted, so once again the pistol is it.

Unlike the wolf, this fellow is a sitting duck. Even though the tranquilizer is taking effect, Emil and the keeper approach the mandrill circumspectly—a tribute to his temperament and power. Something about the way the mandrill looks induces Emil to give him a hefty dose. When it takes full effect the fellow is out cold.

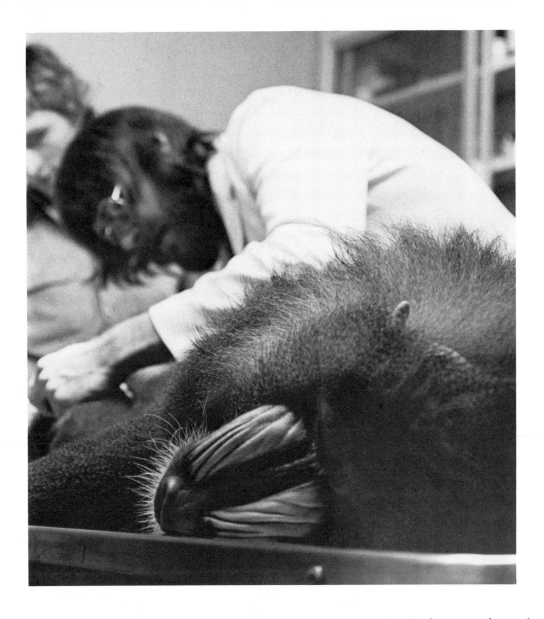

Jim Doherty and two keepers gaze down on the now-helpless animal, each lost in his private thoughts. The mandrill is then brought to the hospital, put on the operating table, and treated for the infected heel.

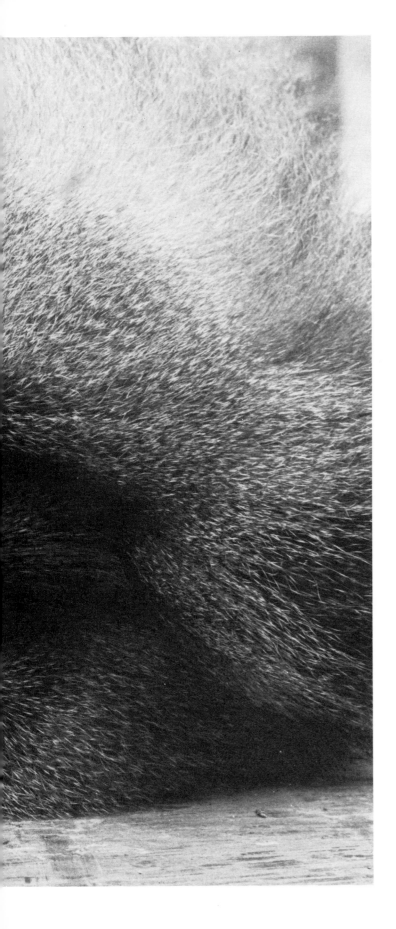

Looking closely at the anesthetized mandrill's face (that's the only way one gets to look closely at a mandrill's face) as he lies on the table, one can appreciate his beauty and grave dignity, violated by the need for medical treatment.

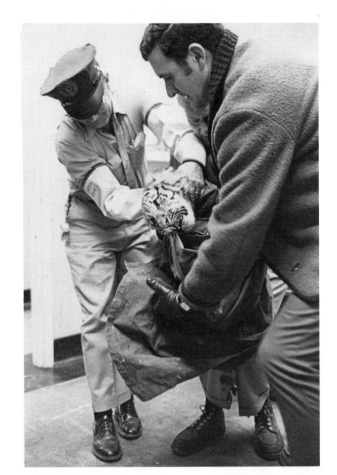

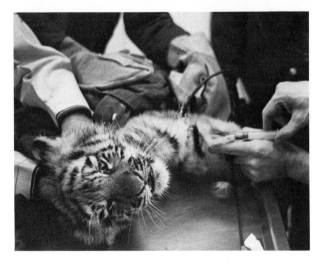

This has been a rough day! No sooner is the mandrill removed than Jim Doherty is back, this time with a four-month-old tiger due for a routine checkup. The first problem is to transfer him from his crate to the examining table. Personnel playing and roughhousing with young tigers have received nasty, albeit unintended, wounds. When such an animal gets panicky he can be dangerous. The keepers don thick protective gauntlets, the crate door is lifted, and a pole with a noose on it is tentatively poked into the cage. For one dramatic moment the keeper and the tiger eye each other warily. Once on the table, with the weight of several keepers holding him in place, the tiger cub seems to adopt a sadly philosophic attitude.

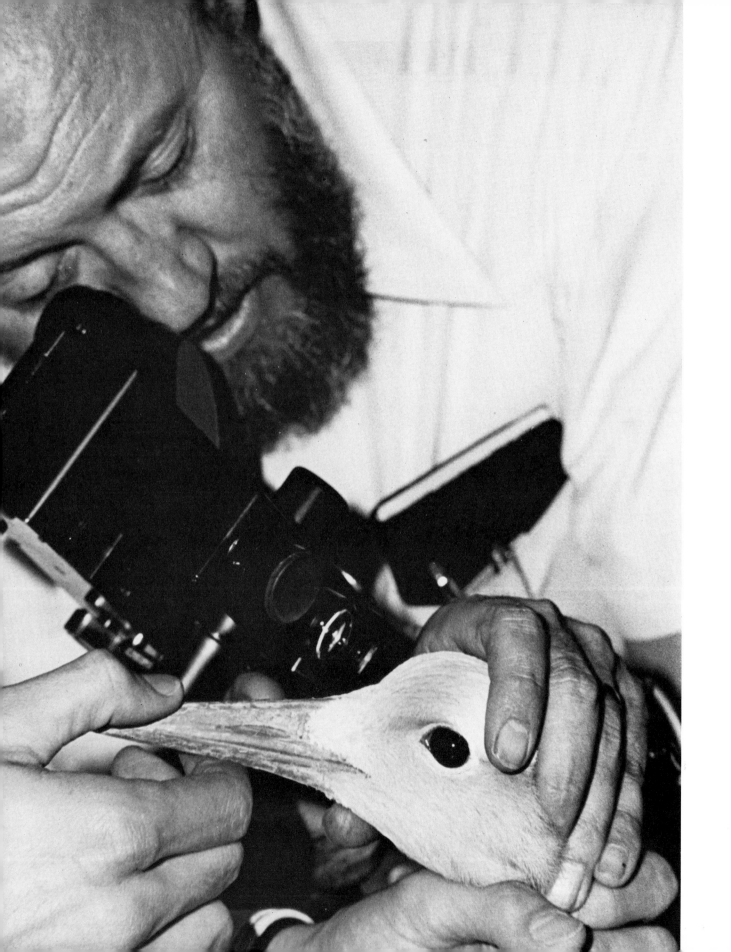

Next comes a succession of birds, most of them with wing or foot ailments. This paradise crane is being treated for a leg injury, and Dr. Bellhorn takes advantage of the opportunity to photograph the fundus of the bird's eye to add to his collection. He probably has the world's greatest accumulation of photographs of the retinal area of various species. This is extremely important in offering potential insights into the areas of comparative anatomy and pathology, since retinal photographs show not only an important area of the visual mechanism but also a representative group of blood vessels and, of at least equal importance, the disk of the optic nerve, which is a direct extension of the brain. The European crane, above, has an infection in both feet following an injury. It does not seem overjoyed when Joe invades its cage and sweeps it up in his arms for transport to the treatment room.

Below, Joe holds the European crane while Emil dresses its feet. The bird seems angry. A day like this when there are a number of problems in the same or related species sends Emil on a detective hunt. He must find out what there is in the animal's environment that might be responsible. He must try to imagine how and why a bird might break a wing or leg.

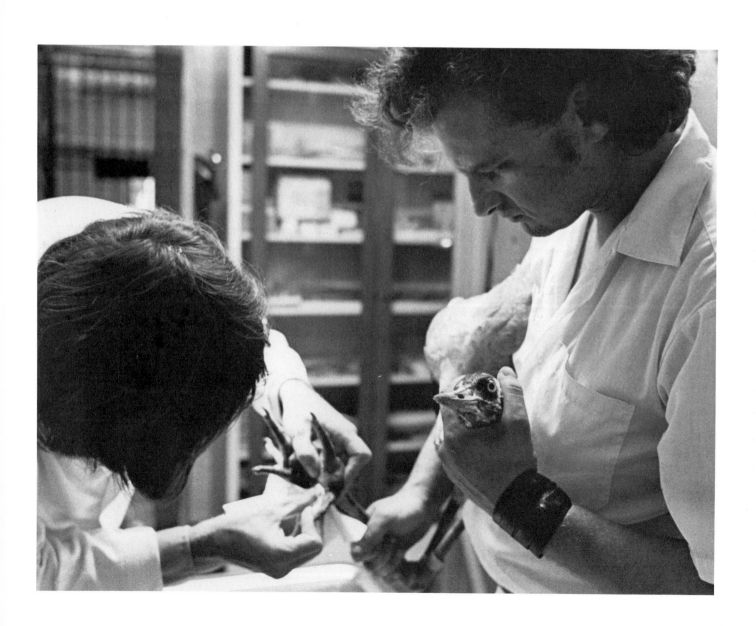

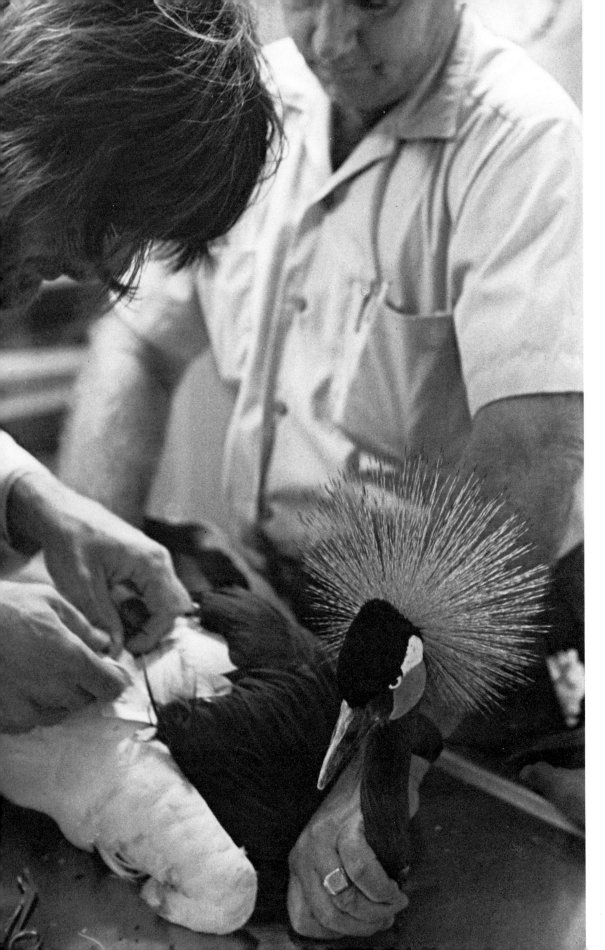

Here Jim Coder holds an African crowned crane while Emil bandages its injured wing.

Emil next goes out to see this bird—an emu. Like rheas, these are large ostrich-like birds, but like ostriches themselves, and unlike cassowaries, they are not often belligerent.

Emil tells a story about his first encounter with emus. Eight of them had to be moved from one enclosure to another. At first the keeper tried herding them into large crates, but they got so excited and flapped around so wildly that it seemed certain they'd injure themselves. The bird people suggested to Emil that he tranquilize them before they were crated. Having had no experience with emus, Emil decided to inject one with a light dose and see what happend. When he walked over to an emu with his syringe, the bird reared in the air and started kicking. Emil took that as a flat rejection and headed for another bird— it did the same. Not wishing to have his block knocked off, Emil retreated and came back with the pistol. Even with the light dose the first bird promptly lay down and went to sleep. Everybody was jubilant, especially Roy, who was there with his fundus camera hoping to get a chance at the birds. Emil and Roy kneeled down to the sleeping bird, got set with the instrument—and that bird suddenly took off about eight feet straight into the air. While they were still kneeling there trying to grasp what had happened, the bird landed back again with a mighty plop, right at their knees. It repeated the procedure several times, so unnerving Roy that he just gave up the project. Of course in the end the birds were properly tranquilized, crated, and transported, but Roy didn't get a chance to look into a single emu's eye that day.

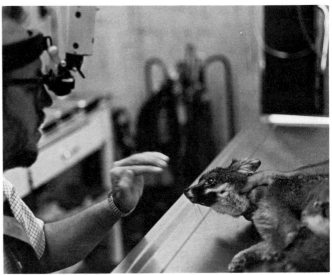

Back at the hospital two more animals have been brought in. The more urgent case is a recently born baby guanaco which seems quite weak. It stands up occasionally, but its legs are too wobbly for it to walk. Emil tries to coax it to walk. Is this one unable because of immaturity or because something is wrong? (Something was very wrong. This baby was unduly weak and, in fact, died some hours later.)

Death is, of course, no stranger in the hospital. Yet it always has a profound emotional effect on the personnel. Here there is no such thing as "getting used to it." Each death casts its pall of failure, depression, sorrow, fear. Meanwhile, Roy is examining the remaining patient, an island gray fox, above. He says he doesn't know whether or not it is ill but it sure has beautiful eyes.

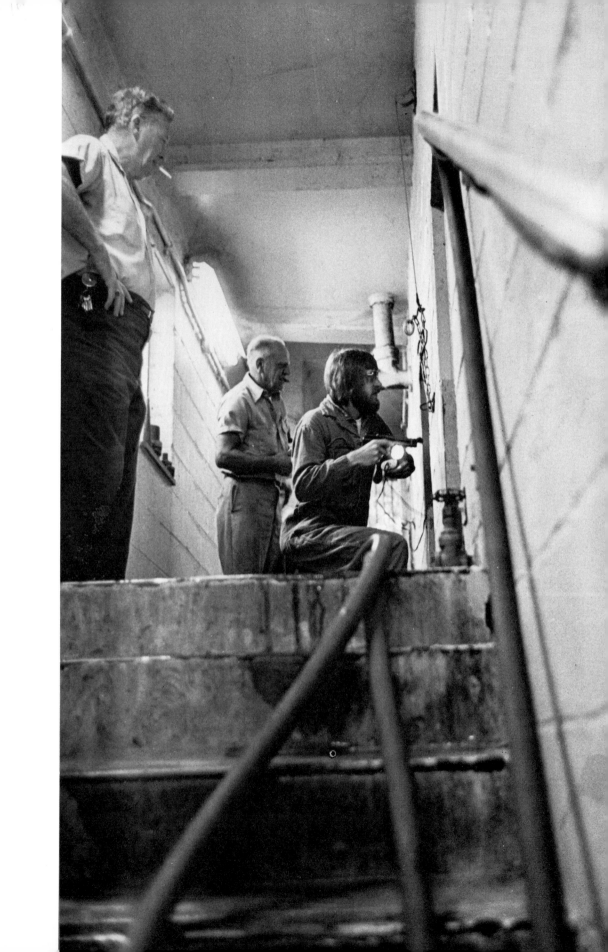

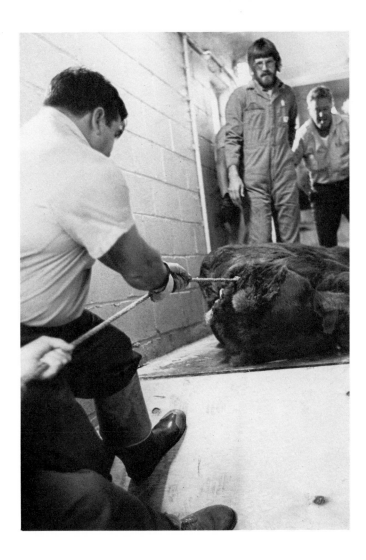

As Emil kneels in the narrow corridor, aiming his pistol, Joe Ruf and a keeper wait until they can approach the animal. The bear is maneuvered out of the cage and pulled toward a ramp that has been placed over the stairs at the end of the corridor.

It would be nice to report that this is the end of a long, hard day. But in fact there remains one chore. A large male Kodiak bear earlier in the day killed a female bear in the compound and has to be shipped out immediately to an animal dealer. A large male Kodiak bear may look funny and cute to a zoo visitor— but he is, in fact, neither. He is serious, dangerous, and imposing. He is the largest land carnivore in the Western Hemisphere. This one must be put in a cage facing the corridor behind the bear exhibit so Emil can get to him with the tranquilizing pistol. A misplaced shot could injure even this huge beast.

At the bottom of the ramp Emil and a keeper help pull the bear out into the open and try to get the bear's head into the metal barrel he is to he carried in. The barrel is a very close fit, and stuffing the animal in is quite a job. Typically, Joe Ruf jumps right into the middle of things. His theory is that there is something in the barrel pushing the bear out while they are trying to push him in. There is—the other end of the barrel. The unconscious bear is finally molded into the shape of the barrel and taken off to the dealer.

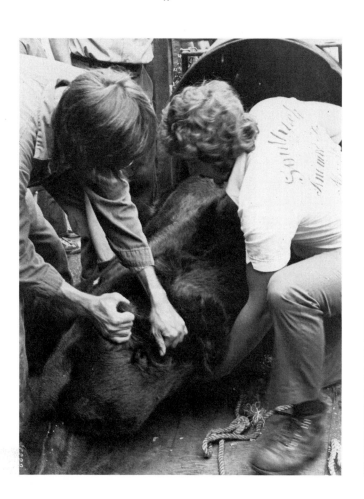

Thursday

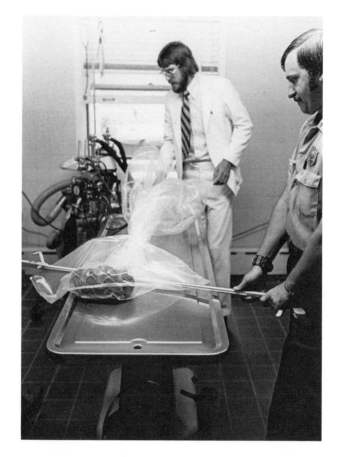

By Thursday morning Emil is tired. No matter. The snake men come in with a Gaboon viper which has amoebiasis. Usually snakes are treated in the Reptile House, where a keeper "pins" the snake and Emil does his thing. These keepers are eminently capable of taking a poisonous snake out of its cage with a snake hook, putting it on the floor or a table, holding its neck down with an instrument, getting it to bite down on a sponge, and then grabbing it just behind the head and holding it safely while Emil examines or treats it. Even in the realm of poisonous snakes, however, Gaboon vipers are not usual. The viper's head is large, about the size of a human fist, and the bones in his skull are so soft and his fangs are so long that he is able to bite right through his lower jaw and catch the underside of the pinner's fingers.

In the Reptile House the viper is removed from his cage with a snake hook and dumped in a barrel lined with a heavy plastic bag. A drawstring is quickly closed. The lid is then clamped on the barrel with a heavy rubber lock, and the snake is brought to the hospital. After the snake-bite kit and antivenin are laid out, Pete and Bob clear everybody from the room, open the barrel, remove the bag and put it on the treatment table.

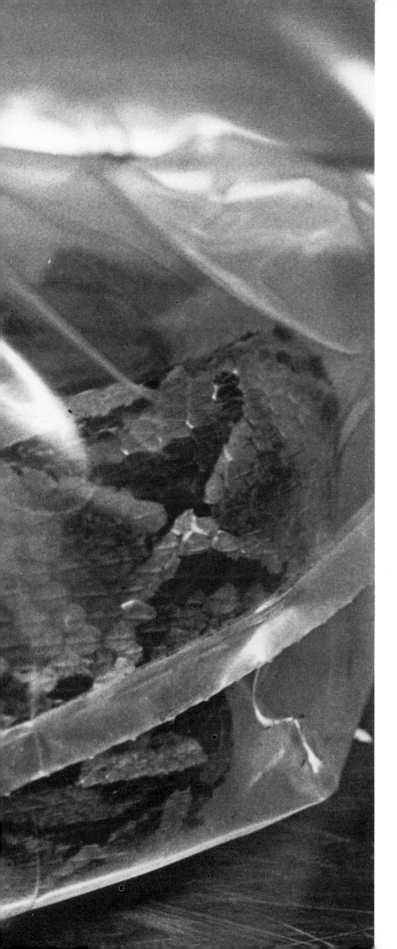

Bob holds the snake bag in position
on the table while Emil adjusts the
anesthesia machine and gingerly
introduces a tube from the machine
into the bag. The snake doesn't
seem to be breathing. Pete says,
"He gets around to taking a breath
every now and then." And so it is.
He takes a breath every once in a
while and eventually stirs about
sensually in the bag. Emil says
that this is the "excitement phase"
of the anesthesia and that the snake
will soon be out cold. Writhing
slowly in his bag, the snake
conveys a sense of voluptuous
beauty and power.

Eventually the snake breathes in enough gas to be fully anesthetized, but even from this point on, the snake men relax none of their caution. Below, Pete inserts a sponge into the snake's mouth and gets a firm grasp of its head. Then Emil introduces a tube into the viper's stomach in order to get a sample of gastric contents for study and to inject some medication. Pete shows a sort of fascination for the viper's fangs protruding from the poison sacs. He measures them, and they prove to be over one inch long.

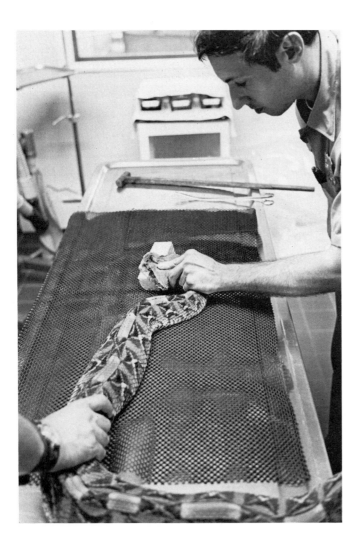
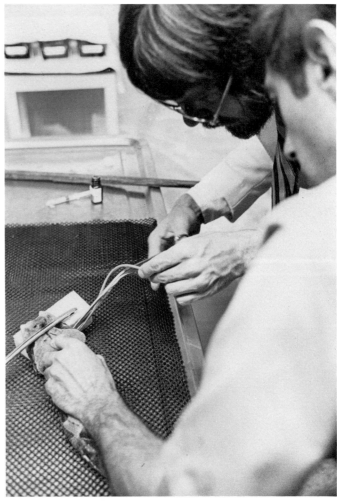

Before he knew what kind of week this was going to be (he "knew," because they're usually like this, but he didn't "realize") Emil had invited a number of children to visit. Emil is very warm and

natural with children, and they never seem to disturb his poise. He just goes on with his work. A dik-dik (a small African antelope) is brought in, in shock, because a pelvic dystocia has prevented her from completing the delivery of a baby she is having. The fetus is dead and the mother quite close to death. With Ian and Nicole watching fascinated, very concerned, and a good bit puzzled, Emil removes the fetus and proceeds to work on the mother. Soon Christian and Christopher join the group, all of them looking pretty anxious. Joe Lombard, holding the dik-dik, left, explains what is going on. The children follow Joe's explanation intently and are greatly sustained by his reassurance that there are laws of nature and that the hospital people can help nature but can't change the basic rules. Joe's patience, clarity, and supportive understanding are remarkable. The dik-dik is treated for shock and put into the incubator. Emil eventually has to do a tracheotomy, but despite all efforts the dik-dik dies within a few minutes.

Emil immediately starts on his rounds, and his first stop is the Children's Zoo, where he has a number of things to do. The Children's Zoo has a varied collection that includes domestic and farm animals and some rather exotic wild animals. A rabbit suspected of having a cold is carefully examined and pronounced healthy. In the background hovers Wayne, a veterinary student at the University of Pennsylvania, working for a month with Emil.

Next is a toucan. When his cage is opened he hops promptly onto Emil's arm, ready to be pleased with whatever comes his way. Pictured on the next few pages is the tamandua (lesser anteater), a cute furry white beast, nocturnal in his native South American jungle, but here ready at any time of day to climb all over anybody who's always wanted to be climbed over by an anteater.

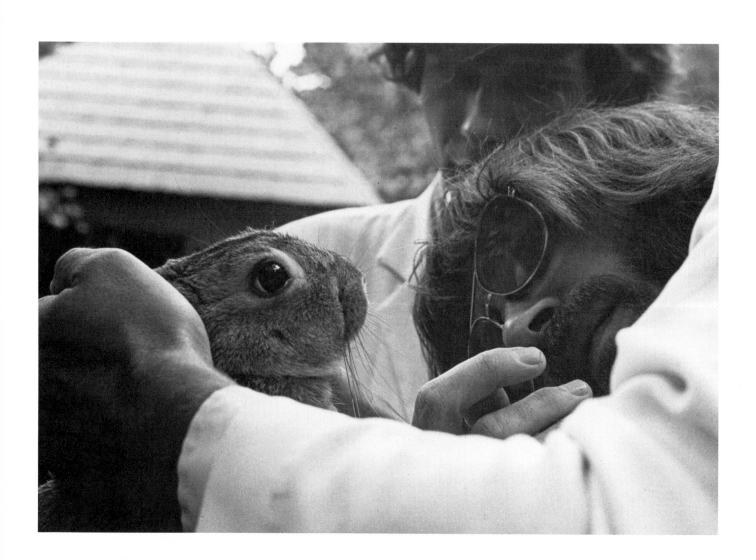

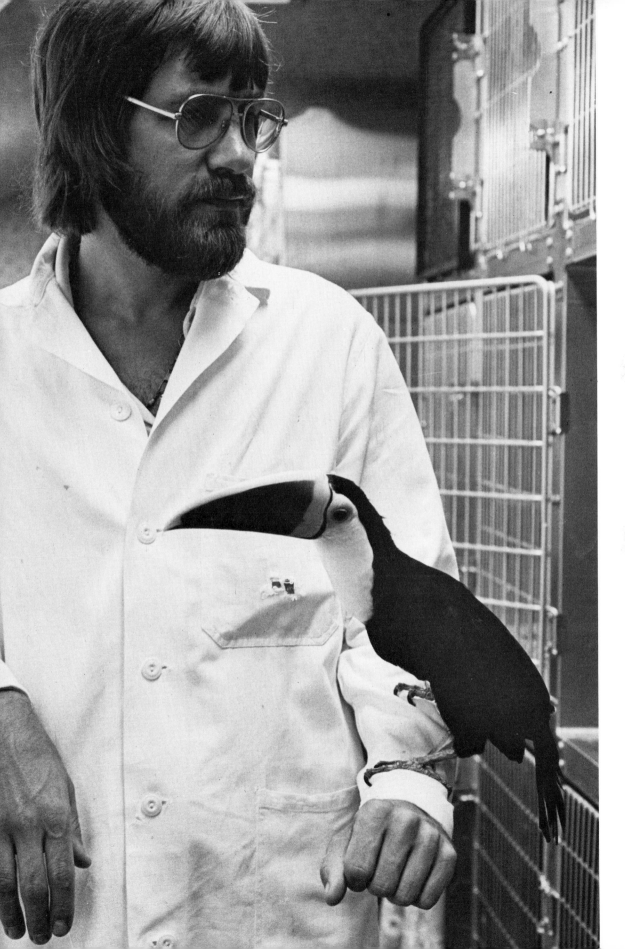

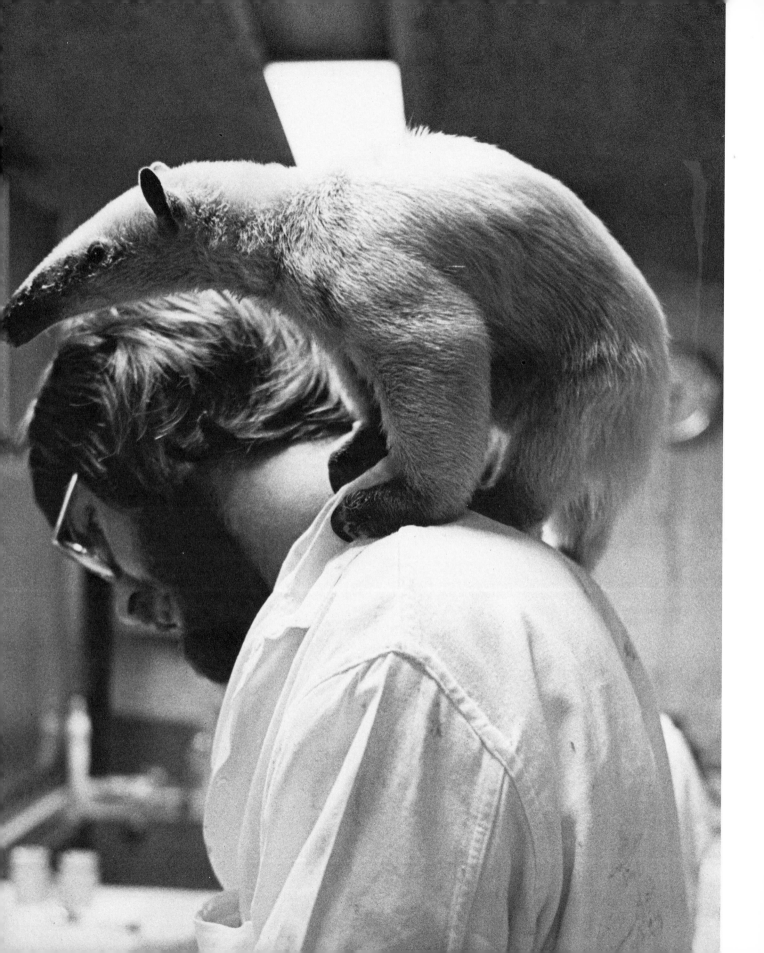

When he is ready, Emil examines the tamandua, which submits graciously, as he does to any kind of handling. He is one of those animals that enjoys physical contact with people.
Although she enjoys the tamandua, Nicole feels much more comfortable when Emil hands her a rabbit which she cuddles with the greatest gusto. The one below is an Angora rabbit with long, silky hair—obviously bred for petting.

The children insist that the guinea pig is beautiful. They admire her facial expression.

While the other children are enjoying the anteater, the rabbit, and the guinea pig, Peter, at two years the youngest of the group, remains fascinated by a large glass tank. Inside the tank is a large scorpion with its babies riding on its back.

After the Children's Zoo the youngsters have to leave. It is just in time too, for a group of scientists are already gathering for the next episode on Emil's agenda. A big male gorilla has become a little lame and shows signs of being under the weather. In studying the problem Emil has made a tentative diagnosis of rheumatic fever and has asked for support from Yale University College of Medicine. Most of the group gathered at the hospital this Thursday afternoon are from Yale. In addition there is Roy Bellhorn with one of his doctors, and a couple of other scientists who need some body fluids for research. Since an animal is tranquilized only when it is clearly necessary for his welfare, maximum constructive use has to be made of this rare occasion. The medical group goes with Emil to look at the gorilla. At first Emil keeps out of the way. Chuma is sitting in relative repose, and Emil wants the group to see him that way. He knows that when the gorilla spots him, the repose will be shattered.

Emil then clears the area and walks in front of the cage with the CO_2 pistol to shoot the gorilla with a tranquilizer. Suddenly, like a bolt of lightning, Chuma leaps across the cage to hurtle into the bars, shrieking a spine-chilling war cry. Then, changing his tactics, he swaggers nonchalantly to the center of the cage and suddenly pauses in a clearly threatening posture.

148

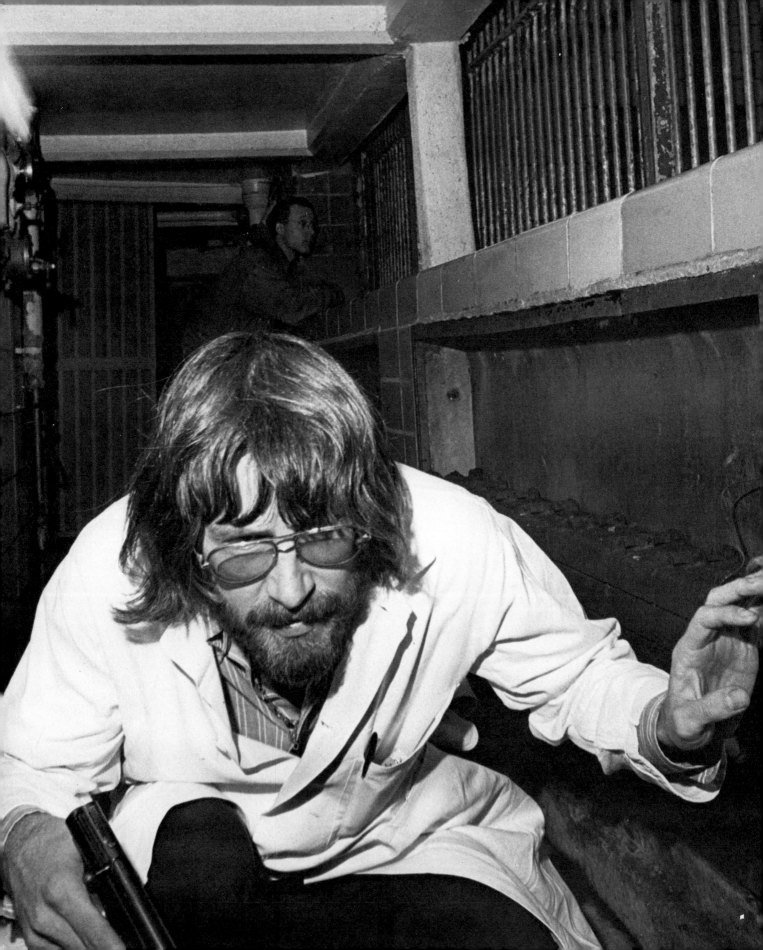

Immediately Emil ducks, knowing from bitter experience that Chuma is planning to resort to artillery. Look over Emil's shoulder as he pokes the pistol through the bars and points it at the dark hulk now in the far corner. Chuma, perhaps meaning to throw Emil off guard, has momentarily turned his back to saunter casually over to a vantage point. That moment is his undoing. There is a soft "plop" and Chuma grabs for the seat of his pants. Before he turns around, Emil has disappeared. The gorilla wanders aimlessly about the cage.

*After a while, with a rather
disconsolate weariness, he shambles
over to a ledge, seats himself
comfortably, and yawns an enormous
yawn. It's too bad the doctors aren't
there. They could at this moment be
making a wonderful study of a
gorilla's throat. Chuma gradually
slumps lower and lower and finally
falls asleep. He looks as though he
were having a rather pleasant dream.*

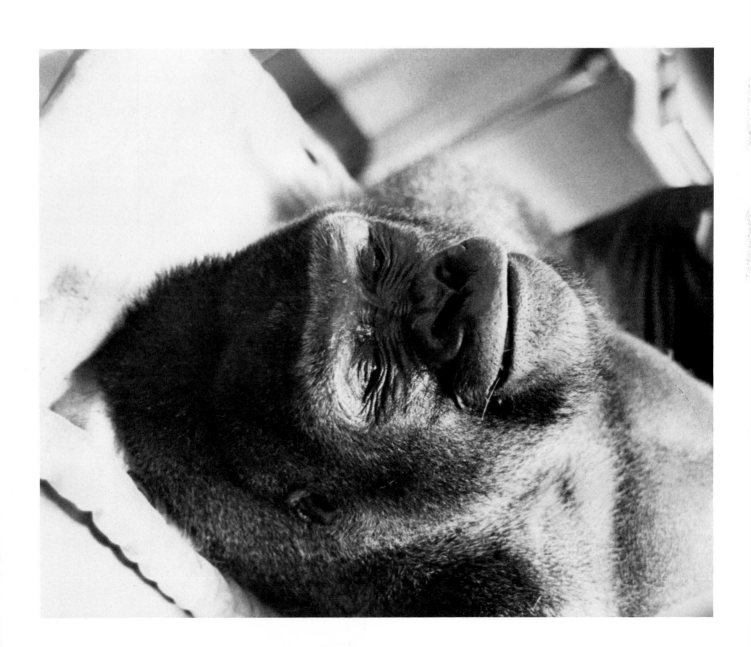

A small group promptly crawls into the cage with a tarpaulin and proceeds to load the gorilla onto it. Chuma is unceremoniously but carefully hauled out and deposited on the floor of the ambulance. Then into the hospital, and onto the treatment table where Joe "arranges" Chuma while Emil and the crew of visitors stand around waiting to get at him.

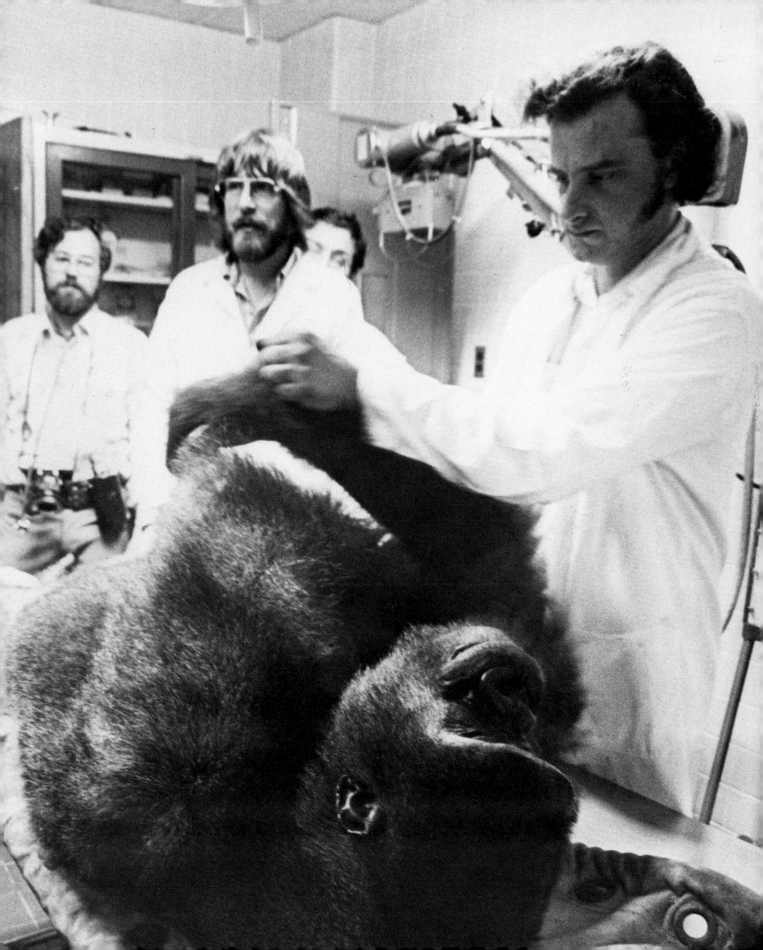

Emil takes a sample of saliva while Joe and an intense lady doctor contemplate the gorilla's huge hand. Even lady doctors don't often get to hold hands with a gorilla.
Dr. Richard Lee, captain of the Yale team, and Emil then check Chuma's throat to be sure his airway is clear, and no sooner do they move away than Roy closes in with his fundus camera.

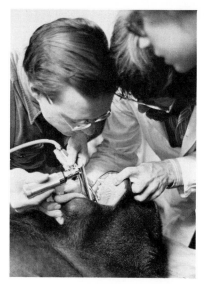

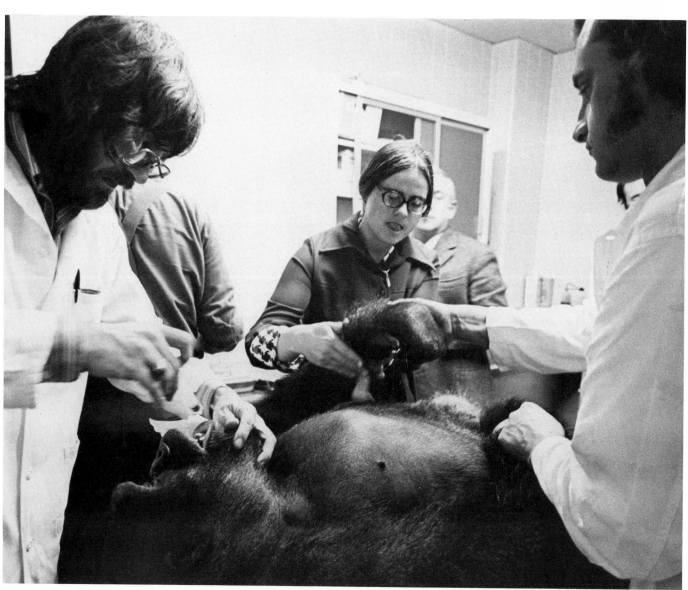

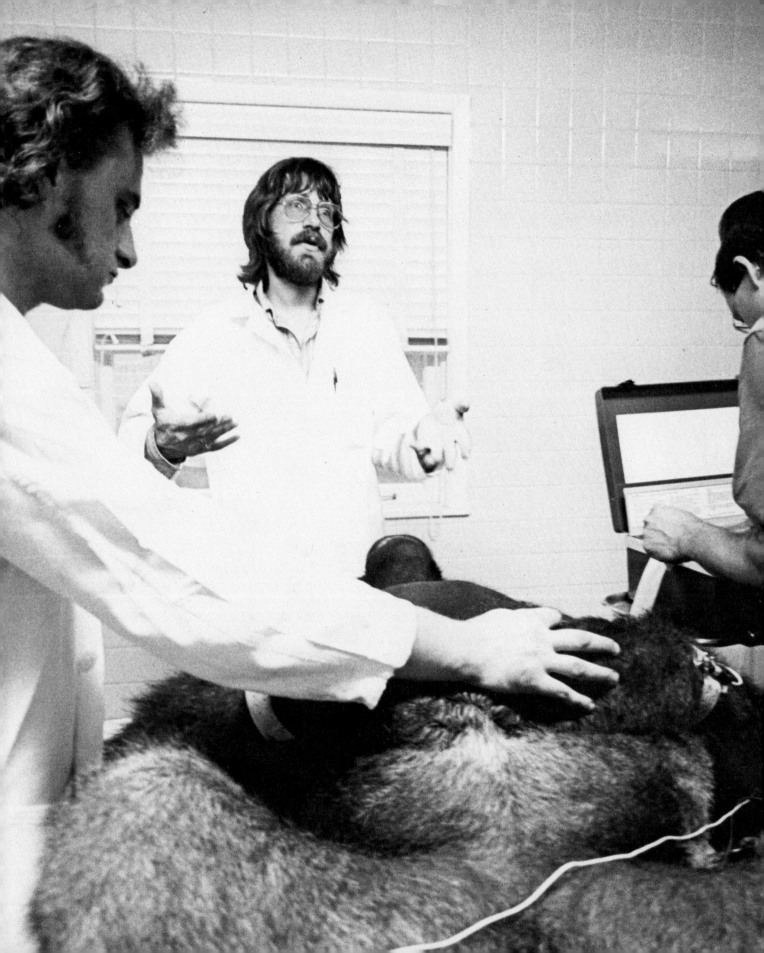

Dr. Lee checks the electrocardiogram tracing while Joe pats Chuma's hand and looks down compassionately. In answer to a question Emil looks as if he were saying, "I can't possibly think of anything else we can do to him." When the doctors have finished and the heavy work has to be done, Joe Ruf and a couple of helpers come in to haul Chuma back onto the tarpaulin, into the ambulance, and into his cage. (It was later agreed that Chuma did indeed have rheumatic fever. He was treated with massive doses of antibiotics, and cured. He still doesn't like Emil.)

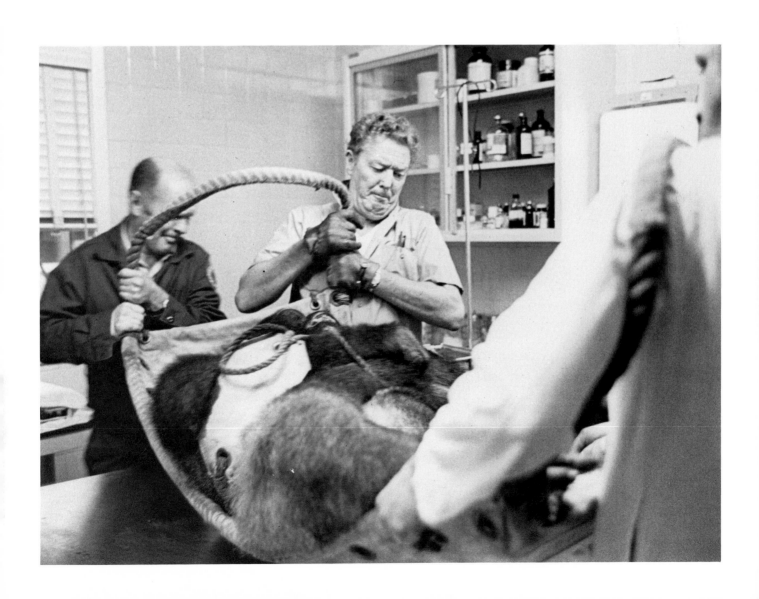

Friday

This morning Emil is able to get right out and start his rounds early. Although no trouble has been reported, some of the bird exhibits are overdue for a visit and are first on the agenda. The beautiful shore exhibit on the opposite page contains several varieties of plovers. The most dramatic aspect of these exhibits at the Aquatic Bird House, as well as exhibits in the World of Birds, is that there is no barrier of any kind between the birds and the public. The birds are completely free. The trick is that each bird is exhibited in an environment so well suited to its needs that there is no reason for it to leave.

This lush tropical exhibit contains numerous waterbirds, such as sun bitterns, stilts, and avocets. The tiger bitterns, opposite, can be aggressive and have been known to wound keepers. They use their beaks and aim for the eyes.

This white-quilled black bustard chick has a leg injury. These chicks are cute and pert, and this one even looks rather bright as Gráinne holds him. From the bird exhibits Emil goes to check the mammal nursery (distinct from the hospital nursery). Two occupants claim his attention but require only routine checks since they are very healthy indeed. Here is what a three-week-old puma in an incubator looks like when faced with a doctor.

At this age, about six weeks, it's hard to say whether a kitten is an ocelot or a margay, though this one happens to be a margay. Either way she is a cute ball of fur, and everyone who sees her wants to hold her, cuddle her, and play with her.

This tree kangaroo shows only mild uncertainty when Emil approaches to examine a rash on his tail. When they're really upset, tree kangaroos rear on their hind legs and raise their forepaws in a boxing stance—just as a human being might do.

Next out to the larger mammals, and it looks as if Emil were doing these in order of size. Zoo yaks need regular tuberculin tests, but they just don't seem to care. Emil handles this one with the aplomb of an old cowhand. When complimented on his rodeo skill, Emil disclaims modestly, "Oh, he's just a young one."

On the way back to the hospital Emil decides to stop for a moment at the Gorilla compound to give an immunization injection to Mopey, a seventeen-month-old male gorilla. Mopey knows what to expect from Emil and becomes very uncooperative indeed when Emil climbs into his cage. His little cage-mate Hodari pitches in as best she can, and Emil decides to do the injection in the hospital. He goes outside and waits in the ambulance while a keeper persuades Mopey to come out with him. When the keeper and Mopey get outside to the ambulance, the baby seems ambivalent. He spots Emil, but he obviously badly wants to go for a ride.

In the hospital Mopey again becomes apprehensive. He keeps glancing around warily, all the while clinging to the keeper. Back in the car, Mopey seems to forget quickly enough. He settles onto the keeper's lap and stares, fascinated, out the window throughout the short ride from the hospital. Any little boy would have done the same.

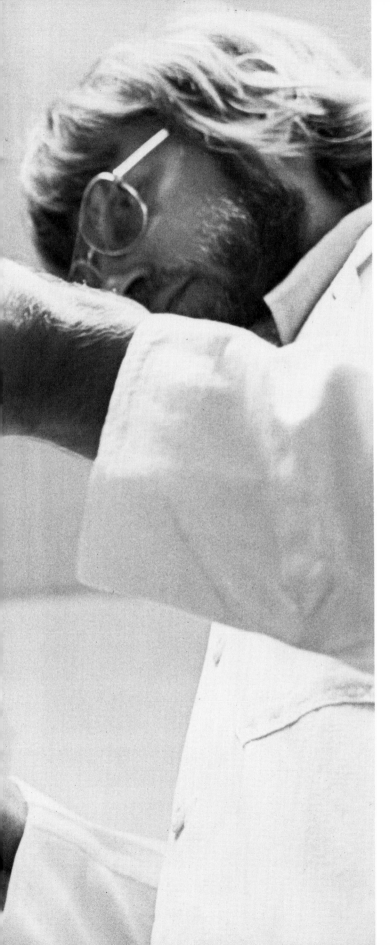

Turning from Mopey to check on the new admissions, Emil finds an old friend. This broad-winged hawk has been in before with wing trouble, and in the ward he showed himself to be one of those birds that has a real need for human companionship and a real capacity for relationships. He was glad to sit on anybody's wrist and would call to passersby to stop for a chat. But he clearly favors Emil and Joe. He shifts his weight from foot to foot in nervous delight when he is on their arms and stands up, erect, proud, and pleased, when he sees that they will let him stay awhile. Some time after this picture was taken, the hawk was sent to the Children's Zoo. Shortly afterward, making rounds, Emil saw him there—and he was a sorry sight indeed. Huddled in the corner of a large enclosure, his head drooping, he barely moved. He not only stopped calling for company, he hardly recognized visitors. His eating had declined almost to zero, he had lost weight, and his feathers looked messy. He was a very sad-looking bird. The diagnosis? Severe depression due to sudden deprivation of meaningful relationships. Emil ordered him back to the hospital, and within a matter of hours he perked up remarkably. By the next day it was almost as though nothing had happened.

Down on the last rung of the size ladder is this tiny beast. For a little fellow who's so easily held in a keeper's hand he has a big name — he's a fat-tailed smithopsis. Both he and the tree kangaroo are marsupials.

After the smithopsis there is a penguin to be looked at. His problem is not emotional—it is very physical. He has a pretty bad case of pneumonia. Although penguins can be excitable, this one is too ill to be anything but resigned. Large doses of antibiotics will set him straight in a few days.

After lunch a large problem presents itself. A Siberian tiger produced a kitten last night, and throughout the day today she has been pacing restlessly in her cage, leaving the kitten abandoned in the inner enclosure. Since a tiger which has just given birth usually dens up with her baby, this is a sign that something is very wrong. The kitten's life is in danger from lack of nourishment, but also, and more immediately, from her mother, who is acting strangely. The curator has consulted with Emil and has decided that the kitten will have to be removed and reared in the nursery and the tiger will have to be brought to the hospital for examination. The atmosphere quickly becomes charged with tension: Siberian tigers are dramatic and valuable animals, and as soon as Emil hears the story he realizes the kitten's life is immediately threatened.

Emil is especially fond of big cats, and this tiger is one of his favorites.

Since it is a beautiful, sunny afternoon, the zoo is crowded with visitors. The Park Police have to clear the area and keep the spectators from crowding in. Emil gets a big dose of a tranquilizing drug into a syringe and heads for the tiger's cage. This tiger is Emil's friend; she will come to him when he calls and will graciously submit to his scratching her. He intends now to call her over and, when she comes, to inject the drug quickly. When he gets to the cage, she bounds over even before he calls. Emil starts to proffer a tentative finger, but the tiger makes it clear she will bite it off along with anything else she can reach. She looks him right in the eye and speaks her piece. Emil takes her at her word and returns to the ambulance for his dart pistol.

Emil is expert with the pistol, but tranquilizing an animal this way is never an easy job. It's not just a question of hitting a large animal anywhere; the animal is usually moving and must be injected in the large muscle a little under and to the side of the tail. The CO_2 charge is quite strong and can do serious damage if the animal is hit from too close a range or in the wrong place. Here is a perfect shot. As the animal stands glaring at Emil from the rear of the cage, the just-fired projectile can be seen hanging from her haunch.

In a moment the tiger leaps to the front of the cage, snarling viciously. Pistol still in hand, Emil starts back in an instinctive gesture of fright.

It is estimated that the tranquilizer will require about twenty minutes to achieve its full effect. Emil moves away to sit some distance from the cage, leaving the tiger undisturbed so she will quiet down. The crowd in the background eagerly waits for the next episode in this impromptu drama. Eventually, the tiger is out and Emil is in.

Jim Doherty and Joe Ruf supervise while Emil takes a blood sample from a vein in the tiger's leg. Joe Ruf is due to retire soon after forty years of service at the zoo. He is in charge of the mammal keepers, and his idea of directing any operation is to take the hardest part of the job himself, to work harder, faster, and better than any of his crew—and to keep yelling encouragement while he does it. He knows how to handle animals and men.

Emil insists that the tranquilized tiger is off on a great trip, although her usually expressive face gives no clue. The crew next has the job of getting the animal to the hospital. A large tarp is spread out to serve as a stretcher, and the tiger is maneuvered onto it. She is then lifted onto the back of a pickup truck and brought to the hospital.

In the hospital, examination discloses that the tiger is producing no milk for her baby, which is reason enough to explain her behavior. While he has her there, Emil removes the tartar from her teeth, a regular routine when large felines are tranquilized. Everyone's attention turns immediately to the baby tiger. Jim Doherty has brought the baby to the hospital, and Jim Coder prepares the incubator in the nursery and puts the little cat into it. The first order of things is food. It is hardly necessary to teach this one to take the bottle. He seems to know what it is and what it is for even before he can get to it.

Next comes a thorough examination.
Everything seems in good order.

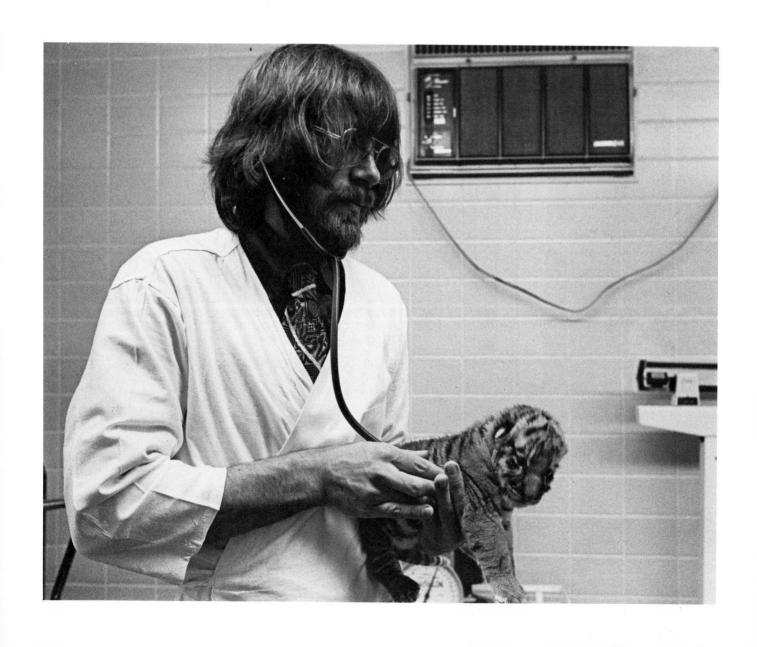

This is the incubator. The large circular flaps are access curtains through which one can reach in to handle or remove the animal.

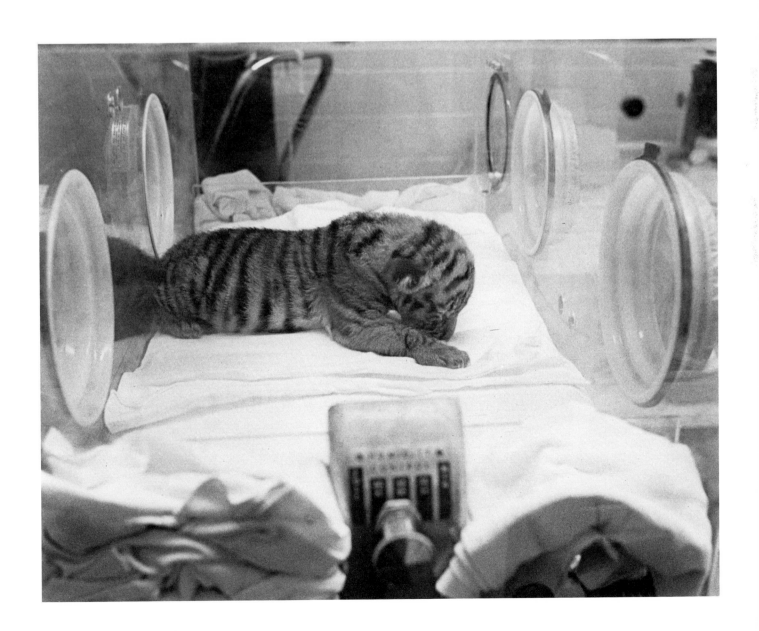

Here is the little tiger in his incubator. Naturally, he doesn't do much but sleep. Occasionally he stumbles around a bit, but at this point he isn't great on locomotion. Now that the job is over, Emil allows himself a moment of luxurious communion with his new charge. Because newborn tigers are delicate, and because this one has been totally neglected for the better part of a day, Emil stays close to it for the next forty-eight hours. He sleeps on a cot in the nursery and gets up every four hours to feed the baby.

And so on into the night.